QUFU

Graveyard

KT-487-598

Old City Wall

Yan Hui
Temple

The Temple of
Confucius

The Kong Mansion

THE HOUSE
OF
CONFUCIUS

THE HOUSE OF CONFUCIUS

KONG DEMAO
& KE LAN

Translated by Rosemary Roberts
Edited and with an introduction by Frances Wood

Hodder & Stoughton
LONDON SYDNEY AUCKLAND TORONTO

British Library Cataloguing in Publication Data

Kong, Demao
  The house of Confucius.
  1. China – Social life and customs –
  1912–1949   2. China – Social life and
  customs – 1949–
  I. Title II. Lan, Ke III. Wood, Frances
  951.04'092'4   DS775.2

  ISBN 0-340-41279-8

Contents

Contents

Chronological Table of Chinese History

Shang	c. 1600 BC–1066 BC	
Zhou	Western Zhou 1066–771 BC	
	Eastern Zhou 770–256 BC Spring and Autumn Period 722–481 BC Warring States Period 403–221 BC	
Qin	221–206 BC	
Han	Western Han 206 BC–AD 23	
	Eastern Han 25–220	
Three Kingdoms	Wei 220–265	
	Shu 221–263	
	Wu 222–280	
Western Jin	265–316	
Eastern Jin/ Sixteen Kingdoms	Eastern Jin 317–420	
	Sixteen Kingdoms 304–439	
Northern and Southern States	Southern States	Song 420–479
		Qi 479–502
		Liang 502–557
		Chen 557–589
	Northern States	Northern Wei 386–534
		Eastern Wei 534–550 Northern Qi 550–577

| | | Western Wei | 535–557 |
| | | Northern Zhou | 557–581 |

| | | Western Wei | 535–557 |
| | | Northern Zhou | 557–581 |

Sui	581–618		
Tang	618–907		
Five Dynasties		Later Liang	907–923
		Later Tang	923–936
		Later Jin	936–946
		Later Han	947–950
		Later Zhou	951–960
		Ten Kingdoms	902–979
Song		Northern Song	960–1127
		Southern Song	1127–1279
Liao		907–1125	
Western Xia		1032–1227	
Jin		1115–1234	
Yuan		1279–1368	
Ming		1368–1644	
Qing		1644–1911	
Republic		1912–1949	
People's Republic		1949–	

Emperors of the Qing dynasty (1644–1911)

Shunzhi	reigned	1644–1662
Kangxi		1662–1722
Yongzheng		1723–1735
Qianlong		1736–1795
Jiaqing		1796–1820
Daoguang		1821–1850
Xianfeng		1851–1861
Tongzhi		1862–1874
Guangxu		1875–1908
Xuantong		1909–1911

THE HOUSE
OF
CONFUCIUS

Introduction

The name of Confucius is known outside China but we know little else of the lowly scholar Kong Fuzi who became a god in his own country and whose views provided the fundamental justification for the system of imperial rule which lasted for over two millennia in China, forming the backbone of the world's longest continuous civilisation.

Confucius, a latinised version of Kong Fuzi ('Master Kong'), was first introduced to the West by European Jesuit Missionaries who reached China in the last decades of the fifteenth century and were overwhelmingly impressed by its social stability, complex bureaucracy and imposing imperial ritual. Even by the time the Jesuits encountered them, the ideas of filial piety and family worship of ancestral spirits, of the essential education of the gentleman-administrator and of imperial rule through the grace of heaven, were two thousand years old.

The continuity of Chinese civilisation owes greatly to the institutionalisation of Confucius' stabilising ideas, and one of its most extraordinary aspects is the continuity of Confucius' own lineage, the Kong family. Elevated and respected, equal if not superior to the imperial household, the lineal descendants of Confucius never moved to the capital to meddle in politics but stayed aloof in Qufu, a small town on a flat plain in the northern province of Shandong where Confucius is traditionally supposed to have lived from 551 BC to 479 BC.

In *The House of Confucius*, Kong Demao, a seventy-seventh generation descendant, born in 1917 and still living in China, describes the extraordinarily privileged yet unbelievably anachronistic life within the mansion of Confucius. Her recollections, told to her daughter Ke Lan, give us an enchanting and enticing glimpse into the private lives and affairs of an ancient and vanished élite. Annual rituals in mansion and temple were based on patterns laid down 2,000 years before; musical instruments were bronze bells and stone chimes, familiar to Confucius but strangely out of date in the early twentieth century when China was discovering the piano, the violin and even the gramophone.

Kong Demao describes how some twentieth-century innovations began to penetrate the petrified mansion: rubber galoshes, whose rain-proofing function was never understood; thermos flasks, admired but unused; and visitors to the mansion today can peer through the windows of the family apartments to glimpse soft, rounded 1930s chairs and couches amongst the hardwood furniture and silk hangings.

Her account of her life in the mansion is particularly poignant for she was amongst the last of the Kongs to live there as the twentieth century finally intruded on the closed world of China's highest nobility. She witnessed the decline of her family's economic and political status and the attempts by various warlord governments, Chiang Kai-shek's Kuomintang and finally the invading Japanese, to co-opt the name, the person, the mansion and the family of Confucius to their own ends. Her brother Decheng, the seventy-seventh generation heir to the dukedom, fled to America and later Taiwan, and the mansion has become an empty shell, peopled only by curious tourists.

Though the cult has finally been officially abandoned, the impact of Confucianism on China is profound. Oddly enough, the Great Sage, a scholar and teacher, was barely acknowledged during his lifetime, ignored by the feudal rulers that he sought to inform. It was not until the Han dynasty (206 BC–AD 220) that his views on private and public morality and the education and conduct of those in power were taken up to become the ruling principles of Chinese government right up until the twentieth century.

Reflecting the period of division in which he lived, for China was then a warring group of small states, Confucius drew on a major theme in contemporary Chinese philosophy, that of man as a social being and his adjustment to society. An almost opposite theme, that of man and his place in nature and the natural world, was developed concurrently by the early Taoist philosophers, and this duality persisted throughout traditional China although it was Confucianism that dominated political thought.

Though Confucius accepted the existence of spirits and of

heaven, he was more concerned with the human world. He stressed the importance of morality in government and the need for rulers to lead their subjects by virtuous example. His belief in the importance of education lay behind the gentlemanly virtues he extolled: integrity, righteousness, loyalty, altruism and humanity. If these were upheld by rulers and bureaucrats then heaven would reward them with its mandate to rule, a mandate that could be withdrawn in punishment. Thus the fall of a dynasty could be explained by the ruler's failure to care for his subjects properly. If all was well in the world, the ruler benevolent and his administrators upright, then the subject would accept his place in society. Confucius believed implicitly in a well-ordered system of acceptance of authority expressed in his famous dictum: Let the ruler be a ruler and the subject a subject; let the father be a father and the son a son. Ritual was also important to Confucius for, properly carried out, he believed that it expressed and reinforced the order within society.

Even in today's China, some Confucian ideas still persist, respect and devotion within the family and respect for education, in particular. It is against the law in Socialist China for children to neglect their elderly parents and the extreme self-discipline in Chinese schools reveals both the institutionalisation and the almost inbred legacy of the Sage of Antiquity.

Such was the continuing power of 'feudal ideology' exemplified by Confucius that during the last years of the 'cultural revolution' (1966–1976), a campaign against Confucius and his feudal thinking was waged throughout Mao's China. Mao's opponents, like ex-Defence Minister Lin Biao were caricatured as 'plotting to restore the Old Order', or bring back Confucianism.

The position of Confucius' descendants is as extraordinary as the tenacious legacy of his ideas. From the time of the Han dynasty, they formed an aristocracy within the aristocracy and their noble position rose through succeeding dynasties until they were virtually equal with the emperors but, as Kong Demao points out, imperial families rose and fell, only the Kong family endured.

The continuity of the Kong family's residence, position and power is surely unparalleled in the world and Kong Demao brings the decaying splendour to life in her detailed account of private lives and personal tragedies. Her account is steeped in the history and folklore of her illustrious family and she mixes legend and history with her own more everyday memories. The mixture of the personal and the historic is very characteristic of China for the Chinese have long cultural memories in which myth and history become part of personal experience.

In Qufu today, this confusion of history and myth abounds. There are so many thousands of Kongs in the area that there is apparently a separate telephone directory to accommodate them. In the Confucian family graveyard, a huge walled enclosure full of indistinct mounds marking the graves of Kongs who died hundreds and thousands of years ago, the bright pink, white and silver paper-flowers of wreaths commemorating a lineal descendant buried a few days before, sparkle against the withered grass of the ancient tombs. The first buildings the visitor sees on the outskirts of Qufu are those of the Qufu Teacher Training College, and though its students led the anti-Confucian movement in the 1920s, the college was originally sited in the tiny town of Qufu precisely because the Sage had always been viewed primarily as an educator. The atmosphere in Qufu was regarded as educationally fertile; ancestral memories linger.

Kong Demao describes how her father successfully got the railway line diverted from Qufu for he feared that the new-fangled 'iron horses' would upset the *fengshui* (wind and water) or favourable siting of the graveyard which could adversely affect the fortunes of the family. Today, Qufu is still some fifteen kilometres away from the nearest railway station and it remains a quiet little country town, its neat streets lined with low grey houses, dwarfed by the towering temple and extensive mansion with its tall trees. Visitors can still stay in a western wing of the mansion and wake to the sound of magpies chattering in the trees of the courtyard.

Though Confucian buildings and the temple dedicated to Yan Hui, Confucius' faithful disciple, still dominate the town, they are now empty of ritual and empty of people. Kong Demao fills the halls with servants and retainers and formal processions with banners and musicians. Behind the rituals of the Sage's birthday and the New Year, however, the traumas of the late traditional aristocracy with its confusion of concubines, second wives and arranged marriages and the loneliness of small children in the dust-filled halls, reveal all too clearly the decay of the old order. The decline of the Kong family parallels that of the last Qing emperors; Madame

Introduction

Tao's apparent poisoning of Kong Demao's mother and her sub-
sequent manoeuvrings recall the despotic and murderous activities
of the Dowager Empress Cixi (1835–1908) who lurked in the
Forbidden City ruthlessly eliminating all who stood in her way.

Despite the grand historic parallels, the private tragedy of
Demao's sister whose husband neglected her whilst squandering her
money; the loneliness of young Decheng, last heir to the title of
Yansheng Duke, left behind in the almost deserted mansion; and the
unspoken misery of Demao's own arranged marriage, are all real,
intimate events, personal miseries that form part of the decay of the
old Confucian order and the birth of modern China.

Frances Wood
Curator in charge of the Chinese section, British Library

1

The Kong Mansion

In a neatly kept street in Qufu, the home-town of Confucius, a palatial complex stands facing southwards onto Queli Road. Dominating the scene is a great triple portal with red-bordered, black-lacquered gates. Above the central gate hangs a gold-lettered tablet inscribed 'The Mansion of the Sage' while to the right and left a gilded couplet reads, 'Sharing happiness with the whole nation, the peaceful, prosperous, respected, glorious Mansion of the Duke', and, 'As long-lived as the heavens, the house of the Learned Sage of Moral Excellence'. The doors are decorated with huge knockers, with brass lion-heads, and a pair of finely sculptured lions sit sentinel at either side of the gate. This, the Mansion of the Yansheng[1] Dukes, the descendants of Confucius by his first wife, was also my home; it was commonly known as the 'Duke's Mansion'.

I am a seventy-seventh generation descendant of Confucius and for more than 2,500 years my ancestors have lived in this road, so my family has come to be known as 'the family of Queli Road'. In the time of Confucius, Queli Road was no more than a small alley on the outskirts of town. The two small, narrow gates beside the main gate of the present Mansion mark the site of the gate of Confucius' original residence. Confucius spent his life in poverty and was said to have lived in a small three-roomed house. Grand halls were constructed later on the same site. As a child I often used to play there. Inside were a dilapidated old carriage said to have been used by Confucius in his journeys from state to state, as well as some of his books and his *qin*, a musical instrument similar to a zither.

Two hundred years after Confucius died, the Han dynasty Wu Di emperor (141–87 BC), acting on the advice of one of his ministers,

[1] Yansheng literally means, 'Continuing the line of the sage'.

the prominent philosopher Dong Zhongshu, adopted Confucianism as the orthodox state ideology and for the first time in Chinese history the philosophy of Confucius achieved a position of importance. From then on the sage was granted posthumous titles by the emperors of every dynasty: the Northern Wei emperors (AD 386–534) named him 'Father Ni the Learned Sage' (Zhongni was Confucius' given name); the Tang emperors (AD 618–907) called him 'Sage' and conferred on him the title 'Prince of Literary Excellence' which the Yuan dynasty emperors (AD 1279–1368) expanded to 'Prince of Literary Excellence and Sagely Accomplishment'. The Ming emperors (AD 1368–1644) named him 'First Master of Sagely Accomplishment', and the Qing rulers (AD 1644–1911) went even further and conferred princeships on the five generations of his immediate ascendants.

As Confucius' honorary titles increased, so too were his descendants treated with greater favour. From my earliest childhood I can recollect family elders speaking of the Mansion as the residence of the Duke, the family of the Sage, 'the first family under heaven', a family even more highly respected than the emperors' families. Imperial families retained their noble status only until the fall of a dynasty, but for the last two thousand years every generation of the family of Confucius had been high ranking aristocrats. By the Ming and Qing dynasties, the Yansheng Duke was even permitted to walk beside the emperor along the Imperial Way within the Imperial Palace in Beijing, to ride a horse inside the walls of the Purple Forbidden City, and to accompany the emperor on inspection tours of institutions of learning. Whenever the Yansheng Duke travelled to the capital he would be preceded by a huge entourage including the descendants of prominent Confucian philosophers and other eminent men and experts in the Five Classics.[1] From the year 1038,

---

[1] Canonical books associated from the Han dynasty (206 BC–AD 220) with the Confucian cult and supposed to have been compiled by Confucius. The truth of this is uncertain but he did refer to the *Spring and Autumn Annals*, the *Classic of History* and the *Book of Odes*. The Five Classics comprise: the *Book of Odes* or *Classic of Songs* which contains poems dating from the tenth to the seventh century BC; The *Book of Changes* (*Yi jing*), a work on divination based on the eight trigrams and sixty-four hexagrams; *Spring and Autumn Annals*, or annals of Lu, the state in which Qufu lay, from BC 722–BC 481; *Book of Rites* and the *Book of History*, a collection of historical documents extending from the Shang dynasty to the late Zhou (*c.* sixteenth century BC–*c.* fifth century BC).

when the Song dynasty Ren Zong emperor granted the forty-sixth generation descendant of Confucius the title of Yansheng Duke, to when my father, as the seventy-sixth generation descendant, inherited the title, it had remained in the family for close to 900 years.

Before the Song dynasty (AD 960–1279) Confucius' descendants had lived in a small house in Qufu, but in 1038 the 'Mansion of the Yansheng Dukes' was first constructed on the same site and expanded during succeeding dynasties. It eventually covered about thirty-three acres of ground, which included gardens, memorial archways and over 460 rooms of varying size and design. Finely carved rafters, upturned eaves and colourful archways, exotic plants and strange stones, cool pavilions and curving bridges made this the largest, most sumptuous aristocratic mansion in the whole of China.

The Mansion was laid out with the Yamen, or administration offices, at the front and the residential section at the rear. Like the Imperial Palace in Beijing it was built along three parallel wings. From front to back along the central wing stood the Yamen offices, the Inner Apartments and the Rear Flower Garden; the western wing included the reception room for receiving important guests, the rooms where the rites were learned, and the studies; and the eastern wing consisted of the Family Temple, the Ancestral Hall and the residential quarters belonging to various relations.

Inside the Second Gate is a memorial archway called the Gate of Double Glory, a structure that only nobles who were granted a feoff were privileged to build in their homes. It stands alone in the centre of the courtyard with a curving, double roof and decorative brackets; eight carved beams ending in flower buds hang down vertically beneath the eaves above white stone drums. The gates were usually kept closed and one had to walk around them; only when the emperor arrived on a tour of inspection or to offer sacrifices to Confucius were they opened to the sound of a thirteen-gun salute. In the course of Chinese history, eleven emperors of the Han, Wei, Tang, Song and Qing dynasties visited the Mansion a total of nineteen times, a mark of imperial respect and favour shown to no other family in China. After the founding of the Republic in 1912, Chiang

Kai-shek[1] and other top Kuomintang officials also made personal visits.

Separated from the western part of the residence by a single wall is the majestic Temple of Confucius. Occupying nearly fifty acres of grounds, its 466 rooms and halls lie amongst ancient trees and memorial tablets. The main hall, the Hall of Great Achievements, stands on a terrace surrounded by a white marble balustrade. A double roof with curving eaves is supported at the front by ten stone pillars exquisitely carved in high relief with twisting dragons, swirling clouds and precious pearls. The workmanship here is superior even to that of the dragon pillars of the Imperial Palace in Beijing. It is said that each time an emperor came to visit, the ten columns were covered with yellow silk so as to avoid annoying him.

The Temple of Confucius also contains one of the most famous buildings in China, the splendid, multistorey Kuiwen Pavilion Library. As a child I became familiar with the line of an old poem often repeated in its praise:

> *A lofty tower rises inside the palace walls,*
> *Ascended by a ladder of clouds one hundred feet tall.*

Here also are the Apricot Altar where Confucius taught his son the rites; the chamber of the sage's wife, Madame Qi Guan; a juniper tree reputed to have been planted by Confucius himself; the Thirteen Stele Pavilions; and large numbers of decorative archways, memorial tablets and other relics, some dating from as far back as 2,200 years ago, when Qufu was part of the State of Lu.

Some two kilometres to the north of the Mansion, along a road lined by ancient cypresses, is the burial ground of Confucius and his descendants – the Forest of Confucius. The fifty-acre forest of cypresses and junipers, surrounded by seven and a half kilometres of walls, is the largest park in China. Hidden deep among the trees

---

[1] After the death of Sun Yat-sen, 'father' of the Chinese republic, Chiang Kai-shek (1887–1975) assumed leadership of Sun's Kuomintang, the ruling party in the Nationalist government, in 1928. Failing effectively to resist the Japanese invasion of 1937, Chiang was eventually defeated in the civil war that followed the end of World War II and in 1949 retreated with his followers to the island of Taiwan.

are over sixty halls and pavilions and thousands of ancient stone tablets. In the past the Temple and Forest of Confucius belonged to and were administered by the head of the Mansion of Confucius.

The administration of the Kong Mansion was traditionally carried out by six departments modelled after the six ministries of the central government, which were located to the east and west of the Great Hall at the front of the central wing of the Mansion. They were the Department of Rites, in charge of ancestral worship; the Department of Music; the Seals Department, responsible for jurisdiction and edicts; the Department of Letters and Archives; the Hundred Households Department, responsible for security work and the administration of the burial grounds; and the department responsible for rent collection and administration of the sacrificial fields – the income from which was set aside to maintain the annual ancestral sacrifices. Department officials were usually grade-four officials on a scale from one to nine (grade one was the highest grade). In addition, there were a miscellany of other officials of various ranks who administered the Mansion or acted as stewards, private advisors, accountants or assistants at sacrificial ceremonies.

The Yansheng Duke proclaimed imperial edicts and attended to important family affairs in the Great Hall located in the centre of the six department offices. In the centre of the hall was a raised platform on which a wooden armchair covered with a tiger skin stood behind a long, red-lacquered desk. Arranged on the desk were paper, writing brushes, inkslabs and ink, the great seal of power, and the arrow-shaped token and small flags that symbolised authority. On either side of the platform were ranged the symbols of a first-grade court official – over a hundred flags and weapons, gongs, parasols, fans, drums and signs bearing the Duke's various official titles and, for use in public processions, signs reading 'Silence!' and 'Make way!'

Behind the Great Hall was the Second Hall where the Yansheng Duke gave audience to officials ranked grade four and above, and where children were examined in rites and music on behalf of the imperial court. Two horizontal boards were inscribed with the words: 'Respectfully inherit the cause of the sage' and 'Poetry, literature, music and the rites'.

The Third Hall was the Room for Withdrawal where the Yansheng Duke handled family disputes and problems involving the Mansion's servants.

But from as far back as I can remember, these three halls had become merely empty display pieces and were never used. When I lived at the Mansion, ordinary family affairs were run by the Bookkeeping Office and the Records Office in the Second Hall courtyard. Just inside the main gate was the Hall for Sending Memorials to the Emperor which handled dispatches to and from the capital. The grade seven county magistrates who came to the Mansion on business had to make their reports here through the official in charge. Without special permission they were not allowed inside the Second Gate.

My elders often spoke of the times when the family were big landowners. During the Qing dynasty they owned some 160,000 acres of land in Shandong, Jiangsu, Anhui, Henan and Hebei provinces, which was worked by hundreds of thousands of tenant farmers. The vast number of tenants made it necessary for subsidiary rent collection offices to be set up in each of the five provinces. Three ranks of collectors operated under a head official; the lowest-ranking of these was responsible for collecting rent directly from each peasant household. Administration of land in other provinces was a particularly complicated business. Various emperors over the centuries had presented parcels of land to the Kong family for the specific purpose of providing funds for the worship of Confucius, and these fields could not be bought or sold. With each change of dynasty, these plots were either augmented or reduced, making it difficult to keep accurate records.

In addition, the Yansheng Duke personally owned some 1,600 acres of private land. Out of respect for Confucius, over 60,000 acres of nominally taxed land and several thousand acres of untaxed land were set aside for the peasants of Qufu, Confucius' home-town.

The sacrificial fields were sometimes farmed by imperially assigned tenants and sometimes rented by individuals known as 'parasitic tenants', while imperial appointees also took care of the watering down and sweeping of the Temple and Forest of Confucius. All these people were considered part of the Kong household and were exempt from doing corvée labour[1] for the throne, but were obliged to work for the Kong family instead. They were named according to their special work as butchers, pig farmers, sheep farmers, cattle farmers, broom makers, sacrifice bearers, duck egg producers, water chestnut growers, scented rice growers, beansprout trimmers and so on, and served the Kong family generation after generation. Apart from those families there were families responsible for supplying fireworks and music for celebrations, birthdays and sacrifices. Some families had the task of supplying guests with tea, supplying boiled water, ice or firewood and others were specially employed to weep and wail at family funerals. This custom of employing 'professional mourners' gradually died out at the end of the Qing dynasty.

These servant households came under the jurisdiction of the Yansheng Duke. Civil lawsuits in which they became involved were handled by the Mansion and special permission was required before matters could be taken to the county government. The Mansion issued its own arrest warrants and had the right to take any of its underlings into custody, try them and impose punishments. The green arrow-shaped emblem of authority in the Great Hall symbolised the power to order a punishment of forty strokes of a flat bamboo cane. The family owned a goose-winged pitchfork, a gold-tipped jade baton and a tiger-tail baton that had been presented to them by the emperor for inflicting punishments. Any of these could be used to put a man to death without the consent of governmental authorities.

There was a Department of Punishments in the Mansion which took charge of collecting unpaid debts. Their duties included pressuring local tenants for unpaid rent, sending letters demanding payment to distant debtors and arresting and holding debtors in custody to expedite payments by their families. In the past, all kinds of instruments of punishment – cudgels, canes, whips and cangues – were displayed in these rooms. Statistics from the time of the Qing

---

[1] In traditional China, apart from paying taxes, men were also required to labour for the imperial government on road-building and repair or maintaining the Great Wall and other construction projects. In the Tang dynasty (AD 618–907) for example, able-bodied men between the ages of eighteen and fifty-nine were required to do twenty days corvée labour per year for the central imperial government, with extra periods for local provincial tasks.

Daoguang emperor record that in 1827, 244 men were employed here, but with the decline of the feudal system, this private penal system also disappeared.

What was the family income? According to old records, at the height of the Qing dynasty, rent alone brought in between 1,900 and 3,800 kilos of silver per annum. Other income came from sales of food and other products and the stipend and gifts bestowed on the family every year by the imperial court. During the Ming dynasty a system of selling official positions was also established by which the court assigned the family an annual quota of prized civil-service posts that they could sell to whomever they pleased for thousands of kilos of silver. The total income was enormous considering that the masters of the residence could be counted on the fingers of two hands.

How was it all spent? The greatest portion was allocated to ceremonies and sacrifices in honour of Confucius; second were gifts sent to the emperor several times a year; and third were gifts to local government officials. In addition, there were the costs of running the Mansion. Although when I was small the family had only four members, there were about 500 hereditary servants. According to the Kong Mansion regulations, if a servant died when his son was still too young to replace him, a temporary replacement was found to serve the family until the son became an adult.

The several hundred servants included fewer than twenty women who worked in the Inner Apartments. The personal maids of the mistress of the house and the top bailiffs held the highest positions among the servants and themselves owned houses and land outside the Mansion. The chief bailiff was rewarded with a village for taking the place of my one-year-old brother, Kong Decheng, in my father's funeral ceremony, 'smashing the plate' and 'mourning with a short walking stick'.[1] Decheng's wet nurse was presented with a

---

[1] Smashing the plate: As the coffin was about to be carried from the hall where it had been resting before the funeral procession, the eldest son of the deceased took a pottery plate and smashed it on the threshold. Mourning with a short walking stick: Direct relatives of the deceased taking part in the funeral procession walked leaning on short walking sticks. The colour of the stick was determined by the relationship of the mourner to the deceased. The eldest son used a white stick.

large vegetable garden. Lesser servants had to address their superiors as sir and madam and serve them as lesser eunuchs served higher eunuchs at court. Generations of hereditary chief bailiffs had developed strong support for the Confucian ethical code. They read the classics, were fastidious over etiquette and wore long gentlemen's robes. The men rode horses and the women travelled by sedan chair when outside the Mansion, and they were often mistaken for the masters of the Kong Mansion themselves. The bailiffs often represented their masters on important business. When my brother Kong Decheng married, his bailiff, Wu Jianzhang, was sent to Beijing to receive the bride, and when my father died it was his chief bailiff Zhao Qing who personally signed the memorial to the Ministry of Internal Affairs announcing his death. Two maids who worked for my grandfather continued to live in the Inner Apartments when my father became Yansheng Duke. They had servants of their own and were treated with the respect accorded my father's elders.

But there was only a small number of privileged servants, and most servants were bound by very strict regulations. Those who served in the Great Hall were not permitted to enter the Second Hall and those who served in the Second Hall were not permitted to enter the Third Hall. Servants were clearly divided by rank, with those of higher rank working further inside the Mansion. Those serving in the 'Eight Houses' (the Inner Apartments, the Gate House, the Bookkeeping Office, the Study, the Hall for Cherishing Ancestral Kindness, the Western College, the Entourage Quarters, and the Outer Western Hall) were treated best and held high offices with good status. Servants of the other sections of the Mansion – gardeners, waiters, and barbers – were all ranked one grade lower. A water carrier received an annual wage of about 500 kilos of grain, while an errand boy of the Great Hall received 325 kilos. Guests attending festivals or birthday celebrations also provided the servants with an important source of income with gratuities that were distributed by the accountant.

Because the Kong family were hereditary nobles, they were permitted to have their own private army. The family Hundred Households Department, also known as the Department of Security of the Forest and Temple, was the equivalent of the imperial Ministry of War and enlisted large numbers of able-bodied men from families under the jurisdiction of the Mansion. After the founding of the Republic in 1912, the Northern Warlord Government provided a security force of over 300 men to protect the Mansion, with 150 troops permanently stationed at the residence. When I was a child, there was only a single company quartered in the Eastern College under a Commander Liu who used to follow us with a small patrol whenever we ventured outside the Mansion.

As the Kong Mansion was the 'Home of the Sage', it had a special organisation to carry out sacrificial ceremonies to Confucius consisting of about eighty masters of ritual ceremonies and 120 masters of music and dance. They only came to the Mansion when ceremonies were to be held and were exempt from other corvée labour. The masters of music and dance were maintained by the Kong Mansion but they did not cost very much. There was a local saying that went, 'Six pennyworth of turnips and a shilling's worth of onions will support a dance master or a musician.'

At the height of their prosperity under the Qing dynasty Qianlong emperor (reigned 1736–1796), the family opened the Fortune and Prosperity Bank, issuing their own currency which was commonly used throughout several counties. The family had a solid financial base and were well trusted. But towards the end of the Qing dynasty, the family began to decline, land holdings were greatly reduced and corruption among rent collectors seriously reduced their income until rent earnings provided only a small fraction of the expenditures. The stipend provided by the court had virtually been discontinued too. According to old family members, the imperial stipend had once run into hundreds of thousands of dollars, but my father only received 2,000 dollars a year. Under such adverse conditions, the Fortune and Prosperity Bank closed down. Yet despite this economic decline, the family still maintained appearances with a luxurious lifestyle. When my father turned thirty, there were ten days of feasting, with thousands of guests partaking of shark's fin, sea cucumber and other such sumptuous delicacies.

2

My Father and Mother

My Father

My father's name was Kong Lingyi and his style (a name taken by men at the age of twenty) was Yanting, meaning 'swallow pavilion'. He became the seventy-sixth Yansheng Duke at the age of five and died in 1919 when I was two years old. He left no impression on me at all, and it was only from the endless stories of people who knew him that I learned about him.

My brother was born after my father's death, so father only knew his two daughters – my elder sister and myself. From his correspondence in which I was often mentioned, it is obvious that he was very fond of me. When I was small I had one photograph that I loved to look at: my father, with a slight smile on his face, is seated in a chair with both hands supporting me as I stand on his knee. This is the image of father that I always recall when I imagine how he had cared for me. After my brother Kong Decheng was born, people often said how closely he resembled the 'old Duke', thus the image of my father became even clearer: a tall, stalwart man with clear, fair skin and gentle eyes. I felt that my own image of father was far more kind and real than the portrait of him hanging in the guest hall.

When my father was young he set up a county school at the Mansion Travelling Lodge in Qufu and established the Four Clans Teachers' College in conjunction with the descendants of Yan Hui, Mencius and Zengzi.[1] He himself took the post of college president. Later he was appointed by the Qing government to inspect educational institutions in Shandong.

---

[1] Yan Hui and Zengzi were disciples of Confucius; Mencius (c. 372–288 BC) was a later champion of Confucianism whose assertion that man is by nature good became a fundamental tenet of Confucianism.

During the reign of the Guangxu emperor (1875–1908), imperial officials were sent to Qufu on four different occasions to make sacrifices to Confucius, and father made four trips to Beijing to wish the emperor long life and thank him for his favours. He received numerous imperial gifts, including calligraphy and writing brushes, 'happiness' and 'longevity' characters written by the emperor, a copy of the *Complete Encyclopaedia of the Four Branches of Knowledge*[1] and silk for long gowns. The Empress Dowager Cixi[2] gave him a mandarin's hat decorated with a peacock feather, an honour highly prized by Qing dynasty officials.

In 1889, father was appointed to the Imperial Academy. The court had a memorial tablet erected in honour of his mother, Madame Peng, and on the death of his first wife sent officials to offer sacrifices. In 1894, when the Empress Dowager celebrated her sixtieth birthday, father took his wife and mother to Beijing to offer their congratulations. The two women each held a breakfast feast for Cixi and hired a theatre troupe to perform three days of opera in the Imperial Palace. Cixi granted them a personal audience, feasted them and presented them with calligraphy and paintings.

After the 1911 Revolution, father was chosen to be the delegate to parliament from our locale, but declined to take the post. President Yuan Shikai, plotting to restore the monarchy, organised the Society for Planning Peace and father was elected an honorary member of the council. He also acted as council head of the Educational Circle's Petitioners' League and represented the educational world in supporting Yuan to become emperor. After assuming the throne as the Hongxian emperor in 1915, Yuan Shikai awarded father with the First Grade Medal and Sash of Auspicious Glory along with an annual salary of 2,000 dollars, and

[1] Although there is no written record of this and the books are no longer extant, several of the family elders recall the gift and claim to have personally seen the Encyclopaedia at the Mansion.

[2] Empress Dowager Cixi (Tz'u-hsi in the Wade-Giles romanisation) 1835–1908, was a lowly concubine of the Xian feng emperor (1831–1861) until she gave birth to his heir. She acted as regent during her son's infancy and continued to dominate him. On his death, she appointed a successor (not in the line of succession) in order to retain control of the court. Famous for her profligate spending (the Imperial Summer Palace is said to have been built with money urgently needed by the navy) and her apparent ruthlessness in murdering rivals, she has become a legend, feared and respected.

later gave him the rank of Prefectural Prince. The forty officials who handled Kong-clan affairs were awarded salaries of 1,200 dollars, and an annual allowance of 2,000 dollars was granted for maintenance of sacrificial vessels and musical instruments. Four thousand dollars per annum were granted for maintaining the security of the Forest and Mansion.

After the fall of the Hongxian emperor, as Yuan had titled himself, the remnants of the Qing dynasty continued to work for the restoration of the Qing emperor. The president of the Confucianist Society (established in Shanghai in 1912), the royalist Kang Youwei,[1] put forward proposals to 'make Confucianism the basis of Chinese life' and 'adopt Confucianism as the state religion'. Father published an open telegram reiterating his policies and pointed out:

Confucianism takes human kindness as its guiding principle, a principle that cannot be abandoned for even a second. For thousands of years, China has built its government, culture, customs and beliefs on Confucianism, and even though our system of government has now changed, human moral principles have not. If China abandons Confucianism, it abandons its very life.

One of the warlords, General Zhang Xun, was a pious Confucianist with a deep respect for the sage. After the overthrow of the Qing dynasty, he refused to cut off his queue (symbolising submission to Manchu rule) and earned himself the name of Queue Commander. My father was a very close friend of his and they became blood-brothers. When Zhang Xun was stationed at Yanzhou he sent troops to protect the Kong Mansion and the Temple and Forest of Confucius. It was also said that father planned to erect a shrine in his honour at Qufu. The site had already been selected, representatives of local counties had met to discuss the project and construction plans were drawn up when Zhang Xun's attempt to restore the Qing dynasty failed. Needless to say, the project was abandoned.

[1] Kang Youwei (1858–1927), a highly respected scholar and radical reformer, one of the key figures in the late Qing, who tried to use a reappraisal of Confucius as a reformer as the basis for China's modernisation.

While visiting Beijing in 1919, father was given an audience by the dethroned emperor Puyi and was granted the privilege of riding a horse in the Forbidden City. He fell ill while in Beijing and died in the same year.

Father had a lifelong love of calligraphy and examples of his art were hung in many places throughout the Kong Mansion. Today rubbings of his calligraphy are on sale in the antique store in Qufu. He loved to paint, and was particularly skilled at painting plum blossoms. I used to have several of his original works, but they were unfortunately lost during the turbulence of the 'cultural revolution'.[1]

Father had a total of four 'wives' including concubines. His first wife, Madame Sun, died of illness, and his first concubine, Madame Feng, failed to give birth to any children. His third wife, Madame Tao, gave birth to a son who died at the age of three, but then she became infertile. Finally he took a second concubine, Madame Wang, who gave him two daughters – my elder sister Kong Deqi and myself – and a son, Kong Decheng. When my father died, mother was five months' pregnant with Decheng. Just a few weeks earlier he had been at home writing letters outlining his plans for the future.

From father's correspondence I pieced together the events of the last few weeks of his life. At the outset, Madame Tao, who had taken my four-year-old sister to Beijing to visit our ailing grandfather, sent a letter to say his condition was improving. Father was delighted at the news and wrote Madame Tao a letter of encouragement and consolation saying that when affairs at the Mansion were not so busy and the old gentleman had recovered, he would come to Beijing for a holiday with them. But two days later, he received a telegram saying his father-in-law had died and hastily left for Beijing to offer his condolences. On the second day after his arrival in Beijing he developed a subcutaneous ulcer on his back. Medical treatment was to no avail and his condition worsened until on November 8 he died in the Yansheng Duke's Mansion in Beijing.

[1] 1966–1976, a period of disruption in which Mao Zedong sought to purify the Communist Party. It involved attacks on all aspects of traditional culture which were seen as bourgeois and reactionary. Many works of art in private hands were destroyed by the young 'red guards' unleashed on elderly intellectuals.

While critically ill, father became concerned about the inheritance of the dukedom and the running of family affairs, and dictated letters to the State President and the abdicated emperor. The letter sent to the President went as follows:

I, Lingyi, terminally ill, prostrate on my pillow, lament as I dictate this valedictory letter. I beseech Your Excellency to peruse my words.

I, Lingyi of eastern Shandong, blunt-witted, mediocre and lacking even the rudiments of learning, inherited my peerage in the second year of the reign of the Qing dynasty Guangxu emperor: after the establishment of the Republic, His Excellency President Yuan showed his munificence in allowing me to retain the title of Yansheng Duke. For the last eight years I have been indebted to successive presidents for their generosity and patronage and after sincere reflection, I can only feel mortified by my inadequacy to requite such kindness.

On October 4, following the death of my father-in-law, Tao Shijun, I came to Beijing to offer my condolences. Here I suddenly developed a subcutaneous ulcer on my back and although I hastened to seek medical care, all treatment proved ineffective and my condition worsened daily. I fear recovery to be impossible.

According to the decrees issued by the Republic, the Yansheng Duke is to enjoy all the privileges he received from earlier dynasties. These decrees also stipulate that the dukedom be inherited by a descendant of the sage; and the name of the successor be submitted to the local chief of administration and ratified by the Ministry of Internal Affairs before the new duke can take office. Approaching fifty years of age, I am still without a son and heir. Fortunately, the concubine Madame Wang is currently over five months with child. If the child is a boy, he should, in accordance with the set practice, inherit the Yansheng Dukedom. If a girl is born, the clan must act to select an heir as they see fit, in keeping with the customs of our ancestors. But my illness is already at a critical stage and I fear I cannot await an heir. Formerly, because of the importance of administering affairs at the Forest and Temple, the Ministry of Internal Affairs appointed a security official, chosen by myself, to act as my assistant. I have already sent a special message to the governor of the province requesting that he appoint Kong Guangda, who was the Dapai County magistrate of Henan Province under the Qing dynasty, to fill the post. Sacrificial rites in the Forest and Temple should be respectfully undertaken by Kong Guangda in the interval until my successor assumes his title, when affairs will be turned over to him. All affairs of the household should be undertaken by my cousin, Kong Lingyu. I beseech you to display your benevolence in approving my request and ordering its implementation, so that affairs will be run smoothly and no damage sustained by the Forest and Temple. Thus not only will my departed spirit in the afterworld be truly grateful, the entire clan will also feel the weight of favours received.

　　Respectfully submitted to
His Excellency the President,

The Yansheng Duke, Kong Lingyi

A similar letter couched in even more respectful terms was sent to the dethroned boy-emperor Puyi.

When father died, his bailiff Zhao Qing sent a letter informing the President and Ministry of Internal Affairs and then made a night trip back to Qufu to inform the clan, while Madame Tao remained in Beijing waiting to escort the coffin home. At the time, Madame Tao's ninth brother Tao Xun was staying at the Kong Mansion. Since his sister's marriage, he had arrogated much of the real power in the Mansion and controlled most of the affairs of the family. He had been an official in Jinan, the capital of Shandong, was a close friend of Zhang Xun, and had intimate contacts with the Shandong Provincial Government. On father's death, Madame Tao immediately sent two secret telegrams to Qufu directing Tao Xun to take control of the situation before Zhao Qing returned. Following her instructions, he locked away all articles of importance, placed a heavy armed guard around the Kong Mansion and asked a prestigious distant relative to come to the Mansion to act as supervisor.

The news of father's sudden death threw the family into a panic, and the problem of finding a successor was discussed endlessly. But Tao Xun already had things under control and kept a very close watch on events at the Mansion. In a secret letter to Madame Tao he wrote: 'Affairs at the Mansion have already been brought under tight control.' Madame Tao's further instructions should be 'secretly indicated to me', who would 'exert the utmost effort to carry them out'. Father had expressed the wish that Kong Lingyu should temporarily run Mansion affairs, but Tao Xun suspected that Kong Lingyu wanted to seize power and sent a warning letter to his sister while Kong Lingyu was in Beijing arranging for transportation of the coffin: 'I don't know whether Lingyu harbours selfish ambitions or not. I beseech you to take great care at all times. Don't be deceived by him . . . I am still making secret enquiries.' In order to increase his control of affairs and reassure the clan, Tao planned to seek Zhang Xun's help in convincing the President to issue an order to shelve the problem of succession to the dukedom until the birth of Madame Wang's child. But the order was never given, either because Tao had at some point changed his mind or for some other reason which remains unknown.

Two months after father's death, preparations were completed for transporting his corpse back to Qufu. To demonstrate his commiseration, the President granted 3,000 silver dollars towards funeral expenses and sent a representative, Wang Da, to offer sacrifices. Another representative, Lu Rongqi, was sent to offer sacrifices to the burial. The coffin returned home by railway in a festooned carriage, with the entourage occupying a first-class carriage and the luggage filling a third-class carriage. Local officials along the route were directed to meet personally and see off the train at the stations under their jurisdiction in order to show their respect for the descendant of the sage.

Father's funeral and interment were a combination of solemnity and ostentatiousness. The coffin, consisting of four inner coffins of Japanese yew and a vermilion outer coffin of cedarwood, was specially transported from Fujian Province. Gold cloth covered the bottom of the innermost coffin and silver cloth was draped over the body. Burial objects (brushes, inkslabs, etc.) and treasures were also placed inside the coffin. The outer coffin was adorned with 'five dragons carrying the sage' – four painted golden dragons coiling around the top four corners and one arching across the lid. During the funeral procession, this was draped with a 'dragon-head, phoenix-tail' red-silk coffin cover. After the body was placed in the coffin, the family burnt paper money and the coffin was sealed. A bier shelter with blue-glass walls and a white-cloth roof was erected in the Qianshang Building Courtyard of the Kong Mansion where the coffin rested for over a year before burial. Arranged before the coffin were tables covered with silk cloths bearing father's name and title, on which were placed paper figures and treasures to be burnt as well as miniature burial objects to be placed in the tomb at burial.

Sixty-four pall-bearers were especially engaged from Beijing to carry the coffin. For a month before the funeral they practised so that a bowl brimming with water placed upon the coffin would not lose a drop of its contents. An overseer stood on top of the coffin directing the operation. To ensure the smoothest possible journey to the cemetery, the road to the gravesite in the Forest of Confucius was rebuilt and buildings obstructing the way were demolished.

I was three or four at the time of father's burial and have only a vague, indistinct impression of what took place, but in later years it was often discussed by the family elders as a major event. Although it was winter and a heavy snow had fallen, people flocked from far and near to see the funeral, many of them spending the preceding night in Qufu's open streets. Their willingness to brave the bitter cold and suffer several days of hardship stemmed not only from a desire to watch the fun, but also from a superstition that had grown up around my father. It was said that whoever set his eyes on the Yansheng Duke would never go blind, so whenever he travelled outside the Mansion he was surrounded by spectators. Now although he could no longer be seen in person, it was believed that even the sight of his coffin would have beneficial effects, and crowds flocked to avail themselves of this last opportunity.

The funeral procession was led by 'path-breaking ghosts', men with pennants, flags, parasols and musical instruments, a troop of horse guards, paper figures and horses, servants to serve the deceased in the afterworld, executioners, *Fangbi* and *Fangxiang*, a paper 'benevolent bestowal pavilion',[1] paper replicas of the former amusements of the Duke (such as birds in cages) and a paper sacrificial altar. On either side of the coffin were sixteen 'funeral-dirge choristers', young boys holding silk cords attached to the bier in one hand and a candlestick in the other. Surrounding the coffin were silk puppets of the Eight Immortals.

---

[1] A paper pavilion containing paper models of gifts from the emperor, or their names written on paper slips.

Directly behind the coffin came the chief mourner, surrounded by a white tent-like cloth. Decheng was barely a year old at the time so his place as chief mourner was taken by the Mansion runner Tu Shigui. Decheng himself was not allowed to take part in the procession as it was feared that it would frighten him. Only when father's body was formally 'invited' to begin the procession to the graveyard did Decheng appear in a servant's arms at the side of the room. My sister and I, like the other women relatives, joined the procession in sedan chairs. There were so many sedan chairs that it took four hours at the main gate alone for all the women to seat themselves.

There were two special ceremonies that had to be completed before burial. The first was a simple ceremony in which the ancestral tablet was consecrated by adding a line to the word 'king' (王) to change it into the word 'master' (主). This was believed to invest the tablet with the soul of the dead. The second was a fascinating ceremony called 'purging the earth'. Before the funeral procession arrived at the cemetery, the Earth-Purging Official led two platoons of cavalry in full battledress and with loaded weapons to the site of the grave where they carried on a fierce battle with the ghosts and monsters until they had all been either exterminated or forced to flee. This ensured that the coffin could be peacefully buried without interference from evil spirits. If the Earth-Purging Official was unable to suppress these demons, disaster and even death was sure to befall him, so it was believed that his task was extremely dangerous, requiring a man with not only social position, but also a strong physique and skill in fighting. At my father's funeral, the Earth-Purging Official was the Yanzhou Garrison Commander. The family treated him with great respect and thanked him with generous gifts of money. According to the regulations, the Twelve Mansions[1] should all have employed Earth-Purging Officials at their funerals, but because of their declining finances, the custom fell into disuse for all but the Kong Mansion.

The day my father was buried, a feast with over 10,000 guests was held at the Kong Mansion. The total cost of the funeral was over 11,000 silver dollars and nearly 20,000 strings of cash.

---

[1] The heir to the Yansheng Duke made his home in the Mansion but his younger brothers were required to live in one of the outer mansions; see p. 92–3.

At the time of the funeral the dethroned emperor, Puyi,[1] issued an imperial edict authorising a contribution of 500 dollars for the funeral costs and sent officials to Qufu to offer sacrifices and deliver a text from the emperor's own study, the Southern Study of the Imperial Palace. Later when my mother was buried at my father's side, the Southern Study supplied the text for the inscription on her gravestone written by the famous Qing dynasty historian Ke Shaomin, who was to be my future father-in-law. But that was still ten years in the future.

To return to the original story, father's death had raised an important question, the solution of which lay with my pregnant mother, Madame Wang. Whether she gave birth to a boy or a girl would determine both who should inherit the dukedom and the immediate question of whether or not Madame Tao could continue to monopolise power at the Mansion. In order to prevent anything from happening to mother, Tao Xun sent guards to watch over her constantly and had a special kitchen set up in the back courtyard of the Inner Apartments where two trusted attendants cooked all her meals. Except for these meals sent to her at fixed hours, she was not permitted to eat anything, and Tao Xun frequently took precautions to prevent the kitchen staff from being bribed. Madame Tao and her brother took great pains to safeguard mother, and mother's fate rested entirely in their hands.

The Birth of the Young Duke

Father had written in his letter to the President that mother was already five months' pregnant and requested that if the child were a boy, he should inherit his fathers' title. But was mother really pregnant? The Ministry of Internal Affairs requested that the Kong Mansion produce a series of documentary proofs before father's request could be granted. Thereupon the head of the clan, Kong

[1]Henry Aisin-Gioro Puyi was the last Manchu Emperor, ruling for three years as the Xuantong emperor (1909–1912). He was deposed at the proclamation of the Republic but later (1934–45) acted as Emperor of Manchukuo, the Japanese puppet state in Northern China. He died of cancer in Peking at the age of 62 in 1967.

Xinghuan, members of the family and Chinese and German doctors all wrote statements to confirm that mother was in fact pregnant.

I found one of the proofs, written by a 'neighbour', Mr Yan, quite extraordinary. How could one of our so-called 'neighbours' (in fact we had no neighbours) give testimony to anything that went on in the forbidden areas of the Mansion behind those high walls – especially since mother never left the Mansion or took part in social receptions when relatives came to visit? Mother was not even permitted to appear at weddings and funerals, so how this neighbour was able to produce proof that she was pregnant I can't imagine.

Nevertheless, the proofs were obtained, the necessary formalities completed, the documents approved and Madame Wang was certified, beyond the shadow of a doubt, to be carrying the Duke's unborn child.

The next question was, would it be a girl or a boy? If the child was a girl, the inheritance of the dukedom would have to be determined by the close branches of the family, and Madame Tao, who would lose her title as duchess, would have to move out of the Mansion along with my sister and me. The clan council soon decided that should mother give birth to a girl, the dukedom would pass to Kong Dejiong of the Fifth Mansion, a child not yet ten years old. Before my brother was born, Madame Tao spent her days burning incense and kowtowing, praying and making vows, in the hope that the child would be a boy.

The Mansion became a hive of activity as relatives from all over the country streamed into Qufu. Their motives were mixed. Some hated Madame Tao and wished to see her out of the Mansion. Some hoped to ingratiate themselves with the family of the potential successor. Most hoped that the child would be a girl, but there were a few who sympathised with Madame Tao out of a deep sense of orthodoxy. In general though, feeling was against her and some members of the clan even went so far as to propose that we should make preparations to move out of the Kong Mansion.

On the fourth day of the first lunar month mother went into labour. Chinese and foreign doctors attended the birth, but the delivery was performed by an old-style midwife – the mother of one of the Kong Mansion errand boys. Father's body had recently been brought back to Qufu and was placed in the Qianshang Building in the Inner Apartments. Mother gave birth in the room behind this. In order to ensure that another baby was not substituted for the real child at birth and to prevent other unforeseen interferences, the Northern Warlord Government sent troops to surround the delivery room and posted guards inside and outside the Mansion under the personal command of a general.

Just before the birth was due, all the old women of the clan arrived to 'supervise the delivery', their sedan chairs completely filling the space outside the main gate. The provincial government also sent an official to the Mansion when labour began. Madame Tao burnt incense and kowtowed outside the delivery room, praying for the 'sage' to descend. In order to receive the 'sage', she had every single door in the Mansion opened from the Inner Apartments to the main gate, including the majestic Gate of Double Glory over which she hung a bow and arrow to ward off evil influences.

It was a very difficult delivery and after several hours of painful labour, the family became very anxious. The old women came to the conclusion that since my mother's last two deliveries (both girls) had been very smooth, this long and difficult delivery would surely result in a 'little Duke'. Some people suggested that merely opening the main gate of the Kong Mansion was not enough, and that the central south gate of Qufu should also be opened to admit the soul of the little Duke. This gate lay directly opposite the Temple of Confucius. It was normally kept closed and only opened when the emperor visited the town on inspection tours or to offer sacrifices to Confucius. After the founding of the Republic, it was opened once when a German envoy visited Qufu and once again when my brother was born. Once the gate was opened, the tense silence was instantly swept away. The errand boys hurried off to get firecrackers, red paper and red silks ready (all symbolising good luck) as if the 'little master' had already been born. Madame Tao, of course, was still waiting on tenterhooks. Later someone pointed out that the Rear Flower Garden, being raised above the rest of the Mansion, was weighing down the buildings in front of it, and that the level of the front buildings must be raised before the little Duke could be born. Consequently a large wooden board with the words

'Lu Ban raised this eight *zhang*'[1] was hung above the corner door of the Back Hall and it is said that only then did my brother Decheng come into this world. The board remained there right up until the time of my marriage.

With Decheng's birth, all of Qufu churned with excitement. A twelve-gun salute was fired and the incessant sound of firecrackers was deafening. At the Kong Mansion, the scene was even more exuberant: runners were sent to notify relatives and the authorities, and men beating drums and gongs paraded through the town proclaiming, 'A little duke has been born!'

At the time feelings in the clan were mixed: some were delighted, some disappointed, some worried and others impartial. As for Madame Tao, the strain had been too much for her and she lay on her bed in a swoon.

When Kong Decheng was born, the head of the Kong Mansion sent telegrams to His Excellency the President, the State Premier, the Minister of Internal Affairs, the Governor of Shandong, and the Governor of Beijing. The text read:

> Madame Wang, concubine of the late Yansheng Duke, who has been carrying his child, on 23rd February, the fourth day of the first month of the lunar calendar, during the sixth watch, gave birth to a boy. Mother and child are both doing well.

An application was also made for the child to inherit the dukedom. The telegrams had just been sent when congratulatory messages began to pour in. Among them was the following telegram from Kang Youwei:[2]

Decheng, My Lord,
    On learning of the passing of our late and most revered Duke, I was overwhelmed with grief. Fortunately an illustrious heir is now born to carry on the line of descendants of the sage. Now the

---

[1] Lu Ban was a legendary craftsman of the Spring and Autumn Period (770–476 BC) from the State of Lu (now Southwest Shandong Province). He was known for creating scaling ladders used for attacking besieged towns and for his milling apparatus. He is traditionally believed to have invented carpenters' tools. A *zhang* is a measure of length.

[2] See note, p. 19.

dukedom can be entrusted to Your Lordship. The noble blood is to be continued in you. When I heard this news from afar, I could not resist feeling an intense joy that drove away my sorrow. I offer Your Lordship wishes for a happy and healthy childhood. I earnestly look forward to the future when you will become familiar with literature and the rites and bring great glory to your ancestors.

With respectful praise,

> Your most sincere servant,
> Kang Youwei.

Other telegrams offered similar sentiments to the family in the child's name.

Soon afterwards, Kang Youwei came to Qufu to see Decheng and I heard that he took great pleasure in holding the baby in his arms.

When Kong Decheng was 100 days old, the Kong Mansion received the following order from President Xu Shichang:

> Twentieth day of the fourth month of the
> ninth year of the Republic
> His Excellency the President confers upon Kong Decheng the
> title of Yansheng Duke.

Thus after elaborate formalities had been completed and the family had endured a prolonged period of anxious waiting, the three-month-old Kong Decheng formally inherited the Yansheng dukedom.

Madame Tao

According to feudal clan convention, Madame Tao, as my father's lawful wife, was considered my formal mother, but when I think of how she tormented and mistreated my real mother and finally drove her to her death, I can never bring myself to call her mother, so we shall simply refer to her here as Madame Tao.

Madame Tao's family came from Shaoxing in Zhejiang Province, but had lived in Beijing for many generations. They had become wealthy and respected although the official posts they held were not high. Madame Tao's father, Tao Shijun, was only magistrate of

Daming Prefecture, so in terms of social status they were greatly inferior to the Kong clan. But because father was a widower who had just acquired a concubine, he couldn't be too choosy. Madame Tao was the fifth daughter in her family and was thus known as the 'Fifth Miss Tao'. She was short, had an oblong face like a winter melon and very rarely smiled. When I was a child, the old people used to say that her features and bearing were all very similar to those of the Empress Dowager Cixi, and when I later saw Cixi's photograph, I recognised this likeness immediately. But it was said that Cixi didn't like her at first because she was not from a high-ranking family. Father's first wife, Madame Sun, was the daughter of the Imperial Envoy, whereas she was the daughter of a mere magistrate. When father and Madame Tao kowtowed before the Empress Dowager after their marriage, Cix asked which family the girl came from. Learning she was a property owner's daughter, she remarked scathingly: 'There are plenty of suitable girls in the families of court officials. Why on earth did you have to choose this one?' Nevertheless, because the wife of the Yansheng Duke had always been named a Lady of the First Rank, Cixi also bestowed the honour upon Madame Tao. Later Madame Tao accompanied my father and grandmother to Beijing to celebrate Cixi's birthday and won the empress' favour by giving presents and hiring an opera troupe to perform for three days at the Imperial Palace. During this period, Madame Tao's daily expenditure on tips alone amounted to nineteen kilos of silver. Cixi was so pleased by this attention that she gave Madame Tao a personal audience, held a feast for her and presented her with many gifts, making her as welcome as one of the imperial family. On her birthday, the Empress Dowager sent her a scroll with the character 'longevity' written in her own hand.

I heard that my grandmother, Madame Peng, didn't like Madame Tao very much either. She would instruct her: 'A Lady of the First Rank must be sedate of bearing and gentle in speech.'

She was renowned in the Kong Mansion for her fierce and insidious brutality, and the people of Qufu nicknamed her 'the Tigress'. The appropriateness of this appellation can be seen from the way she treated my mother.

My mother, whose family name was Wang, was the daughter of an impoverished peasant from Zunhua County in Hebei Province. As a child she had been sold as a servant girl to the Tao family in

Beijing, where she was given the name Baocui – 'Precious Jadeite'. When she reached the age of sixteen or seventeen disaster struck – two of the sons of the Tao family took a fancy to her and argued themselves to an impasse. At this time, Madame Tao and my father were visiting the Tao family after their marriage, and in order to settle the family dispute, Baocui was sent to the Kong Mansion with them.

By the time my mother reached the age of twenty, my father was already forty-three and still lacking an heir. According to traditional belief, of all the actions which violated the code of filial piety, none was more serious than to die without leaving a son to carry on the family line. Having no sons was particularly serious for the Kong Mansion, as it presented complicated problems with regard to the inheritance of the dukedom. In order to solve the problem, mother was raised to the rank of concubine.

When Madame Tao was at home in Beijing, she was accustomed to beat and scold mother, but after moving to the Kong Mansion and being named a 'Lady of the First Rank', her temper became even more violent. Particularly because father was fond of mother, Madame Tao's tyranny reached unprecedented levels. In the freezing cold of the winter, when father had left Qufu on business, she would order mother to take off her clothes and kneel naked on the floor where she would beat her with a whip. She kept a special whip for this purpose, consisting of many narrow leather strips fastened to a six inch wooden handle. A single blow of the whip would raise numerous welts.

Madame Tao would beat mother until she was tired and then made mother kowtow to her and express her gratitude. Mother always meekly resigned herself to this maltreatment and never put up any resistance. With father away on business, Madame Tao was free to torment mother just as she pleased. No one dared to interfere and even while mother was pregnant Madame Tao continued to abuse her as usual.

Sometimes Madame Tao would beat mother inexplicably, as if it were a compulsory duty that she had to carry out. Once when she was going to Jinan, she had completed all the preparations and was thinking over what else had to be done when she exclaimed: 'I almost forgot to beat Baocui!' Thereupon she called mother into the room, curtly ordered her to kneel down and began to beat her viciously. Only when the beating was over would she board the train.

There was a certain Grandma Peng, a relative of my own grandmother, who was a very upright woman accustomed to speaking out, of whom Madame Tao was somewhat afraid. Consequently, whenever she came to the Kong Mansion to visit her relatives, mother's beatings would become less frequent. Whenever Madame Tao beat her, one of the old women of the Inner Apartments would quietly ask Grandma Peng to come.

Mother met very few of the family relatives – distant or close. Not only did she not mix with family members coming to attend funerals and weddings, she was not even permitted by Madame Tao to meet women relatives who called at the Inner Apartments. My mother was at the Kong Mansion for over ten years, yet saw virtually no one.

The old women servants of the Inner Apartments, Mother Jin, Mother Zhu, Mother Zhang . . . were all very fond of my mother and addressed her with terms of endearment, treating her like one of their own daughters. Each time she suffered a beating at the hands of Madame Tao they would wait until her oppressor had gone and then steal in to comfort her. They were the only people who knew the way Madame Tao treated mother; neither the hundreds of servants who worked outside the Inner Apartments nor those living in the Twelve Mansions had any clear idea of what went on. But with the passage of time, rumours began to spread. Some people believed them and others didn't.

Although she abused mother each day, Madame Tao was careful to burn incense and worship the Buddha. She longed ardently to have a child and directed the majority of her prayers to the Goddess of Mercy, the Bringer of Sons. But although the images of these divine beings were constantly supplied with offerings and wreathed in incense smoke, they never sent her a single child.

Of course, we three children were all considered hers, so Madame Tao was the mistress and we children the junior master and mistresses, the joint 'rulers' of the Kong Mansion. My mother, though a concubine, was in fact treated worse than a servant. While mother was in labour, Madame Tao sat cross-legged on her bed in her own room waiting, and when we were born, we were carried into Madame Tao's room and given to her. Relatives all came to congratulate her as if she had been the real mother. From then on we were reared by a wet nurse and no further notice was to be taken of 'Baocui' who had been ordered to call us 'master' and 'miss', as though she were just another of the servants.

All the affairs of the Mansion were ultimately handled by Madame Tao. The head of the Bookkeeping and Records Office of the Mansion was a man named Du Bingxun whom she had brought with her from her family's house in Beijing. He was her trusted henchman and kept the Mansion's accounts. Madame Tao made us call him step-father. After his arrival, Secretary Du became very wealthy. He built a house for himself and took in a concubine, but later came to grief: Madame Tao discovered that he was exceedingly corrupt, threw him out and made him leave Qufu. When he left, no one examined his baggage with the result that he made off with a large cache of valuables from the Mansion. But he hadn't imagined that Madame Tao would set an 'ambush' for him on the road. His convoy was stopped and checked and all his belongings were confiscated, leaving him in desperate straits. Obviously, when it came to dealing with Madame Tao even he had to acknowledge that he had more than met his match.

Madame Tao also brought several other people with her from Beijing. Apart from Secretary Du, there was the Secretary Chen Wencai, a carriage driver, gardener, and other servants, as well as a number of her brothers. Ninth Uncle, Third Uncle and Eleventh Uncle were all frequent visitors and always stayed at the South Flowery Hall, the residence reserved for honoured guests. Many of the affairs of the Mansion passed through their hands – they controlled building construction and the purchase of materials, social gatherings and the giving of gifts. They concerned themselves with everything in the Mansion and although clan members complained among themselves, no one dared to say anything openly. Madame Tao meanwhile sat before a desk in the Front Hall each morning, listening to business reports and rendering decisions on all sorts of requests and petitions. From my brother's birth until the time of Madame Tao's death, officials in the Mansion had to address petitions or letters: 'May the Honoured Mother and His Excellency the Duke graciously grant . . .' Clearly Madame Tao was determined to maintain her authority in all aspects of Mansion affairs.

After coming to power in the Mansion upon the birth of Decheng, Madame Tao became very active in the clan and in society. She made plans to revise the family register – the first time in 2,500 years that a woman had undertaken this job. Preparatory work had been in progress for two years, and formal work was about to begin when she took ill and died.

A red horizontal tablet with gold characters reading 'Boundless Kindness Extending Afar', which had been presented to Madame Tao by the citizens and gentry of several counties near Qufu, hung in the Front Hall of the Inner Apartments. As the story goes, when an army once passed through Qufu, Madame Tao sent them wine, meat and other gifts with a request that they refrain from disturbing the area. As a result the military officers ordered their troops not to occupy the people's homes and not to molest or loot. After the army had gone, the officials of several counties presented Madame Tao with the horizontal plaque and a pair of couplets carved on wood,[1] the exact inscription on which I have forgotten, though the general sense of it was to eulogise Madame Tao's great righteousness in enhancing the 2,000-year-old customs of her ancestors, her pains-taking care in raising the young sage and her bestowal of favours on the townships. According to the couplets and tablet, Madame Tao was without a single fault.

In contrast to this was a letter of complaint written to the Prime Minister by Kong Xianbiao and other representatives of the Kong clan's sixty households. It ran:

Madame Tao is of petty and low birth, and exceptionally jealous by nature. Madame Wang, concubine of Kong Lingyu, the late Yansheng Duke, gave birth to a son and a few days later died a suspicious death. Du Bingxun and Chen Wencai are both sons of evil officials of the Qing dynasty Ministry of Punishments, so it is beyond our comprehension how they can call Madame Tao 'sister' and illegally occupy the Mansion. They move about as

[1] A major form of architectural decoration in China was the addition of decorative wooden boards over a door (horizontal tablet) and attached to the columns on either side of a door (paired couplets). These boards were carved with inscriptions, often of a poetic nature, carved in the style of a famous calligrapher. Both the content and the style of the calligraphy were important aesthetic considerations.

they please and eat and drink at the Mansion's expense . . .
Firewood from the Forest and Temple totals approximately
500,000 kilos a year, and was originally the common property of
the Kong clan; but Du and his henchmen have supported
Madame Tao in claiming it all as her own, in removing the
surplus and in not permitting the clan to gather it for their own
use. Recently they have also forcibly seized the site of Kong
Fandian's tomb and committed acts of evil far too extensive for us
to enumerate in full here.

Yet this letter and others like it were powerless to weaken the
position of Madame Tao. She ruled the Confucian Kingdom
undisturbed until the time of her death.

According to the family rules, no male guest was permitted to
spend a night inside the Inner Apartments. At the time of the
Constitutional Reform Movement in the late 1890s, Kang Youwei
came to Qufu to propagate his ideas, and was later invited several
times by his friend Kong Xianglin (a close relative of the Yansheng
Duke) to write a preface for a book about stone-carved inscriptions
in the Forest of Confucius. Each time he came he stayed in the
Southern Fifth Mansion at the home of Kong Zhaozeng, never
staying at the Kong Mansion or entering the Inner Apartments. But
after my father died things changed. Zhang Zongchang (a local
warlord) came to the Mansion along with his ten coquettish jewel-
laden concubines and over a hundred 'hairy troops' (actually
Russians), and created a great stir. Unexpectedly, Madame Tao
broke all precedents and invited Zhang and his concubines to stay in
the Inner Apartments. The Russian soldiers roamed freely throughout the Mansion and even into the Rear Flower Garden which was
normally the exclusive domain of us three children. The 'hairy
troops' picked the flowers and stripped the trees as they pleased. At
the time, the pomegranates had just ripened and they pulled them
down, took a few bites, skin and all, and threw them on the ground.
The inhabitants of the Mansion and members of the Kong clan were
outraged and expressed their disapproval. But of course such
protests were all carried out behind Madame Tao's back and no one
objected openly.

Madame Tao's action was proof that there was no ordinary
relationship between the Kong Mansion and Zhang Zongchang.

Father had been his sworn brother and after father's death, Madame Tao had taken us three children to Jinan to bewail our 'bitter fate' as widow and orphans. Zhang gave us financial aid several times and once donated 20,000 dollars for the building of the Rear Hall in the Temple of Confucius. For the huge project Zhang had timber shipped by rail from the Northeast to the Yao Village Station, where he organised a large group of labourers to transport it to the Mansion.

Zhang Zongchang visited the Kong Mansion and my father's grave many times and was responsible for providing the security troops who protected us. When Decheng reached the age of six, he and Zhang's son, Zhang Jile, became sworn brothers at his father's urging. At fourteen, Zhang Jile was the regimental commander of the First Model Youth Regiment in his father's Army of Righteous Prowess.

Mother's Death

On the seventeenth day after Decheng's birth, my mother was poisoned by Madame Tao.

In a feudal clan in which a 'mother takes her rank from her son', the birth of the 'little Duke' could not fail to raise mother's social position, but this was something that Madame Tao would never stand for, a fact that mother herself was well aware of. On the third day after the birth, Madame Tao ordered her trusted subordinate Kong Xinquan to prepare a prescription of Chinese medicine said to cause extensive bleeding leading to death in women who have just given birth.

Ordinarily if someone in the Inner Apartments was ill, Doctor Liu Mengying was asked to treat them. Never before had anyone been given medicine by Kong Xinquan. Furthermore, my mother's post-natal condition was perfectly normal; on the day she died, the Kong Mansion had sent a telegram to the Department of Internal Affairs in Beijing reporting that 'mother and child are both fine'. But suddenly Madame Tao brought a bowl of medicinal soup to mother, saying she had been shivering in her sleep and must drink it. This abnormal behaviour roused mother's suspicions. She fully understood Madame Tao's actions and had anticipated that she might try to poison her. By coincidence, one of the old servants, Mother Tang, witnessed the whole scene: mother knelt on her bed imploring Madame Tao not to make her take the medicine as she was not ill. Madame Tao was of course unmoved and insisted that she drink it. After mother had drunk the medicine, Mother Tang remained constantly at her bedside in a state of great distress. Mother said to her: 'Were I to live, my life would only be misery. I'm not afraid of drinking the medicine, it's just the children . . . I'd love to see the children.'

But even this humble request was not to be satisfied, for mother saw none of us again. My brother Decheng had been taken away from her when he was born and she never set eyes on him again.

After mother's death, Madame Tao issued a statement saying that she had caught a chill when being moved from the delivery room to where she was to convalesce. On Madame Tao's orders, mother's coffin was quietly carried out through the back door of the Inner Apartments late one night. She was buried in an overgrown corner of the Forest of Confucius with just a pile of yellow earth to mark the grave.

The family discussed mother's death privately, never in public. Their motives for this were mixed. In such a large family, there were people who dared to speak out in the name of justice, but who lacked concrete evidence; these people are beyond criticism. But there were those who before Decheng's birth had plotted to gain advantage by courting the possible inheritor of the dukedom; their silence grew out of thwarted ambition and total indifference to my mother's tragic end. Although these relatives basked in glory as descendants of the sage, hypocritically supporting feudal moral standards and flaunting loyalty and filial piety, their motives were entirely selfish. But in the face of power and authority they were, of course, always cowed into silence. As far as moral integrity went, those blindly loyal old servants who occupied the lowest positions at the Kong Mansion were far more pure than any of their lot.

But among the ranks of the several hundred servants and errand runners, there was a single rebel. About ten days after mother's death, one of the errand boys ran away. The evening before, he had been seen at work as usual, but the next morning he had disappeared. Only later did we learn that he had gone to the provincial authorities in Jinan to report on his superior and request that an inquisition be held into mother's death. I can't imagine how he found his way to Yanzhou in the darkness, and how from there he boarded the train. That was a time when:

The Yamen gateway faces south, gates open from within,
Though reason's just, without a fat purse, you can't get in.

Arriving in Jinan, penniless and powerless, it is amazing that the provincial authorities paid any attention at all to him, especially since Madame Tao's ninth brother was an official in Jinan. Yet this brave man finally triumphed in his bid to see a wrong redressed, for the provincial government agreed to send officials to the Kong Mansion to investigate. This lucky event was in fact related to the political situation at the time. After the May 4th Movement in 1919, the campaign to 'overthrow the cult of Confucius' curiosity shop' reached a peak and government officials split into factions, one supporting and one opposing the movement. The anti-Confucian officials sought to make use of this case to increase their influence, and after setting up a file to investigate the cause of Madame Wang's death, sent two officials to Qufu. This was no trivial matter and Madame Tao was greatly alarmed. According to the old servants, when the provincial officials arrived at the Mansion, she collapsed on her bed in fear. But this woman would never resign herself to any easy defeat, and she continued to plan her insidious countermoves. The first questions the provincial officials asked were about the prescription, and Madame Tao took the opportunity to find a scapegoat. Kong Xinquan had not only written out the prescription but had also bought the medicine, and at his confidential briefing with Madame Tao there had been no third person present who might act as a witness. Thus Kong would find it hard to vindicate himself – he was the perfect victim.

Madame Tao's ruthlessness was well known throughout the clan and Kong Xinquan was well aware that even if the provincial government didn't bring him to justice, Madame Tao wouldn't allow him to live much longer and might possibly seek to silence his whole family. Trapped in such a situation with no way out, Kong Xinquan committed suicide by swallowing opium.

After Kong Xinquan's death, Madame Tao was still hypocritical enough to visit his family and offer condolences, but in front of all the guests, Kong Xinquan's wife told her exactly what she thought of her and the 'Lady of the First Rank' left in great embarrassment.

After Kong Xinquan's suicide, the provincial government announced that with 'a life for a life' the case was considered closed, but what methods and how much money Madame Tao and her brother in Jinan used in achieving this end are unknown.

When Madame Tao poisoned my mother, my sister Deqi was five. I was two and Decheng was not yet twenty days old, so she left no impression on us at all; thus I only came to know her through her photograph, a large portrait that hung in her old room, the west room of the Qiantang Building. The picture showed her to be a regular-featured, kindly, gentle and submissive young woman. I remember as a young child of three or four, gazing up at her portrait, quite unaware that I was gazing at my own mother.

As a child I knew nothing of motherly love or family warmth. But as I grew up I came to know who my real mother was through my old wet nurse, Mother Wang, and through her quiet narrative, broken at frequent intervals to wipe away her tears, I learned much about mother's life.

After birth, each of us was cut off from all further relations with mother and carried to Madame Tao's rooms, where a wet nurse took care of us. From then on, Madame Tao became our formal mother. We called her 'Mother' (*niang*), addressed Madame Feng as 'First Mother' (*dama*), and called our own mother 'Second Mother' (*erma*). At home the word 'Ma' didn't mean mother, but was used in the names of married women servants. Although mother lived near to us, she was not permitted to kiss or fondle us, and was not even allowed the liberty of giving us fond looks. She could only stand respectfully before us with downcast eyes and address us as 'Elder Miss' and 'Second Miss'. How did she feel at such times? She was thinking of her children even as she drank that fatal dose of medicine, yet she had never once touched them.

An aged aunt from the Fifth Mansion, four generations older than me, told me that mother actually had physical contact once with my sister, Deqi. When mother was pregnant with Decheng, Madame Tao beat her so severely on one occasion that the old women servants were afraid for her life. They didn't dare intervene personally, but instructed my elder sister to run in and seize Madame Tao's whip. If she failed to grasp the whip, she was to throw herself onto mother to protect her. Four-year-old Deqi did as she was told. As mother knelt on the ground, my sister clung tightly to her neck, calling her 'Erma', or 'Second Mother', quite unaware that she was embracing her own mother. Since she was such a young child, the incident left no impression on her, but my mother must have remembered the incident until the day she died.

According to the old servants, mother lived a lonely life, for she was neither one of the masters of the house nor one of its servants. At first she lived near the small Buddhist temple, but later moved to the western part of the Front Hall. She would eat alone in her room – two dishes per meal – for of course she was not allowed to eat as well as we did. Her food should have been taken to her by a servant, but she often went to the kitchen to fetch it herself, and perhaps to ask for a little salted vegetable. The old cook was one of the few people who ever saw mother, and reported that she was tall, wore her hair in a bun, spoke in a gentle voice, and frequently did what was usually considered servants' work. Everyone, with the exception of Madame Tao, treated her well.

Madame Tao was insanely jealous of the tender regard that grew up between my mother and father and used every conceivable means to prevent father from visiting mother's room. If she discovered him in her room she would follow him there and make a scene, while mentally recording it as a debt that mother would have to pay. But fortunately father was not often at home then. When father was dying in far-off Beijing, he often thought of mother and me and sent a letter asking for our photographs. Madame Tao sneered at him: 'With one foot in the grave you still haven't forgotten your little concubine!' When mother and I had our photograph taken, I sat in the centre while she stood behind me to one side. Although I was only two, I was the 'young lady' while mother was just a servant girl turned concubine. We could not possibly be treated as equals.

When I revisited Qufu last year,[1] I found this photo of mother hanging in the west room of the Qiantang Building. It had been cut out from the photograph of the two of us and enlarged as an individual portrait. This was the only photograph ever taken of her.

Although all we knew of mother came from other people, deep in

[1] 1979.

41

our hearts we still cherished a sincere and instinctive love of her. Mother's kindhearted, graceful image made a deep impression on our young souls. I remember once when we were all very young, my sister and brother and I discussed how in the future we would build a proper tomb for mother, both to set our own minds at ease and to provide mother with a beautiful home where she could rest peacefully ever after.

When I was thirteen, Madame Tao died, and preparations were made to bury her next to my father. A kindhearted member of the family suggested that since mother had done a great service to the Mansion by bearing the seventy-seventh generation duke, the three of them should be buried together. Never before in the history of the Kong Mansion had a concubine been buried alongside a duchess, but it was finally agreed upon. When the family council made this decision, my brother was so moved that tears filled his eyes and he fell to his knees before the family and kowtowed in grateful thanks. At the time he was only eleven years old.

A Forgotten Woman

Early each morning, a tall, thin, melancholy young woman slipped into the Qiantang Building, and standing in the centre of the main room, called in a low voice, 'Is Madame Tao up yet? I wish Madame good health.' After receiving an answer, she would silently slip out again.

This was the concubine whom I have so far only mentioned by name, our 'First Mother', Madame Feng. According to regulations governing concubines at the Kong Mansion, she had to pay her respects to Madame Tao every morning. Apart from this, at New Year, on the first and fifteenth days of each lunar month, and at the beginning of each of the twenty-four solar terms, she had to kowtow to the lady of the house. On each of these occasions, she would stand submissively before Madame Tao with her eyes on the ground and say: 'Today is the first day of the month [or whatever day it was]. I kowtow to Madame.' After kowtowing she would take three steps backwards with her eyes still lowered, turn around and leave quietly.

Her life was also very tragic. She was a concubine, but was

infertile and not particularly beautiful, so she neither evoked Madame Tao's jealousy nor suffered her curses and beatings, but rather passed her life in melancholy loneliness. She was the daughter of a merchant, and, it seemed, had never left the Mansion since the day she entered it. According to the Kong Mansion rules, an infertile concubine was not permitted to enter the main hall casually, and apart from obligatory courtesies, she never entered the main hall and very rarely left her room. Thinking back, besides repeatedly paying respects and announcing her kowtows, I don't ever remember Madame Feng saying anything else.

After Madame Tao poisoned my mother, in order to give the impression that she treated the concubines well, she began to allow Madame Feng to attend receptions. The family had never before seen the unknown woman seated beside Madame Tao, but she needed no introduction, for a single glance was enough to appraise her status. She wore a pale magenta skirt and sat on a low stool beside Madame Tao. According to Kong Mansion rules, concubines were not permitted to wear bright red or green skirts, but had to wear pale magenta, and in the presence of the mistress of the house, were not permitted to sit on a chair, but had to sit on a low stool.

There were many other Mansion rules governing concubines. When the mistress died, concubines had to wear mourning like a son or daughter. They were not allowed to address family relatives as 'uncle' and 'aunt' but had to call them 'master' and 'my lady'.

After poisoning mother, Madame Tao upset all precedents in her efforts to fool the public by allowing Madame Feng to live in my mother's old bedroom, the west room of the Qiantang Building. Madame Tao lived close by in the east room and Madame Feng waited on her hand and foot like an old servant. She spent the whole day running around at Madame Tao's command, bringing tea, pouring water, always silent. She would often go to the kitchens to fetch Madame's food or pass on her instructions, and the kitchen staff thought she was a new servant.

When I was eleven years old she took ill and died, still a young woman.

Of course, in the history of the Kong Mansion and Kong Clan, there were concubines who rose to positions of power, bullied the mistresses of the house, and even drove them to suicide. But even if the family rules had been stricter, there still would have been certain individuals capable of attaining enough power to rise above all rules.

Kong Lingyi, father of the author

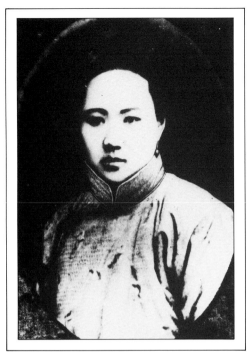

Concubine Wang

Madame Tao

The author with her sister Kong Deqi (left) at the age of thirteen

Seated left to right are Kong Deqi, Kong Decheng, Madame Tao and the author. Nurse Wang is standing at the back.

Kong Lingyi and Madame Tao (back row) with Madame Peng, the
author's grandmother (on the right, front row)

3

Life In The Inner Apartments

Forbidden Palace

The thirty-acre Kong Mansion, containing over 460 halls and pavilions, had only four masters – Madame Tao, my brother, my sister and I, all living in the Inner Apartments.

Entering the main gate and following along the central axis of the Mansion, one passed the Second Gate, the Gate of Double Glory, the Great Hall, the Second and Third Halls, and six courtyards before arriving at the gate leading to the Inner Apartments.

The Inner Apartments were the forbidden zone of the Kong Mansion and entrance by the unauthorised was strictly prohibited. In the past, a notice hung over the gate which read:

> Internal affairs of the Mansion are of critical importance, no man whatsoever may freely enter at will. Light offenders will be prosecuted, and serious offenders will be severely punished without mercy.

Among the hundreds of servants who worked inside the Mansion, less than twenty had access to this area. Outside the gate were two rows of gleaming weapons: goose-winged pitchforks, tiger-tail cudgels, golden-headed jade clubs, all like the props in a Beijing Opera. But this was no performance. It was all to guard the sanctity of the Kong Mansion. These weapons served as a warning to anyone that might be rash enough to force his way in.

As a result of this policy of restriction, particularly to male servants, there was once a great fire in the Mansion, probably during the reign of the Guangxu emperor (1875–1908), which began when bed drapes were set alight by a candle. Few people were in the Inner Apartments at the time, most of them women, while the people outside were either too far away to be aware of the fire, or heard the cries for help but didn't dare enter the forbidden zone. As a result, the fire gradually spread, burning for three days and three nights and reducing seven wooden buildings to ashes. The rising hot air carried burning embers into the sky which could be seen from beyond the Mansion walls. The local people said that this was a 'fire from heaven'. At the time there was no fire brigade, water was in short supply and the source a long way off, so everyone was at their wits' end. The Qufu County Magistrate knelt for three days before the fire begging the God of Fire to show mercy. Finally a method was found to combat the flames. Several piles of cash were heaped on the ground and it was proclaimed that whoever brought two buckets of water and poured them on the fire could take as many coins as he could grasp in one hand. Several errand boys were given the special task of adding more cash to the piles. People came from all over Qufu County to carry water and put out the fire.

When I was small, the old people often spoke of the great fire. They claimed that more money had been spent rebuilding the Kong Mansion after the fire than had been spent constructing the town of Qufu during the Ming dynasty – and that did not include the cost of replacing calligraphy, paintings and valuables lost in the blaze, or the piles of coins used to pay the water carriers.

After this fire, Qufu established a fire brigade called the Heavenly Raiment Society with headquarters in the vicinity of the Drum Tower. In the early years of the Republic, another fire broke out in the Kong Mansion in one of the schoolrooms, but because it was discovered early, it was put out the same day.

Despite the outbreak of several fires, the problem was not solved. Water in the Inner Apartments remained inadequate and male servants were still forbidden to enter. Not even the water carriers who supplied the Inner Apartments were allowed inside the gates. There was a stone water trough next to the main gate which ran through the wall into the inner courtyard. Water was poured into the trough and flowed into the forbidden zone.

To the right and left of the main gate of the Inner Apartments was a long, black lacquered bench on which were seated the dozen or so gatekeepers. Whenever an important guest arrived, they would stand in a row with hands at their sides while the captain announced in a long, drawn-out call: 'My Lady XX has arrived!' Then one of the maidservants would come out and either receive the guest or politely turn her away. When I was small there were seven runners on duty at the gate – four to guard the gate and three to forward news, but by this time Mansion rules had been relaxed and the three of them were permitted to enter the Inner Apartments to make their reports.

Originally, these gatekeepers had both a ritual and protective role to play and had to strictly observe etiquette. But when I was living at the Mansion, there was a strange man called Han Dekui who, when on guard duty, would squat like a statue in the doorway never moving an inch. When important guests arrived he took no notice, but continued to squat with a blank expression on his face. In over ten hours of guard duty, he would not drink nor even relieve himself, and from that point of view there was no one more loyal to his post than he. His superiors never criticised him and everyone called him 'Gate Squatter'.

According to Mansion regulations, if important guests arrived by sedan chair they had to dismount at the Small East Gate next to the corner tower and change to a special Kong Mansion chair in which they were carried into the Inner Apartments. This chair was small and light with a single seat and a blue felt cover. It was carried by two bearers and was only used inside the inner courtyards. Each time Madame Tao left the Mansion she would ride one of these small chairs from the door of the Qiantang Building to the Small East Gate where she would change to her carriage and catch up with the escort. The escort's job was to follow in attendance whenever the master or mistress of the house travelled outside the Mansion. When they were not so engaged, they would rest inside the Entourage Quarters. Since the escorts went everywhere with their masters, their physical appearance was considered extremely important and had to match that of their masters. My father was tall and strong, so his escort was composed entirely of men of similar build.

Madame Tao's trips outside were highly complicated affairs. When she mounted the chair inside the Inner Apartments, in addition to the two bearers, she required a footman to support the carrying poles. As she passed each gate, the gate guards stood in a row and respectfully welcomed or bade farewell to her, while their captain stepped forward to pay his respects. After receiving respects at several gates, Madame Tao would finally arrive at the corner gate where she would mount her carriage. Leading the procession was a mounted footman known as the 'outrider' whose duty was to clear the way. In the evening, there were men ahead of him to the right and left carrying lanterns printed with red characters reading 'Mansion of the Yansheng Duke'. Following the outrider were a minimum of eight armed soldiers from the Kong Mansion Security Department and finally behind them came Madame Tao in her carriage. The carriage was exquisite. The saddles were decorated with enamelware and the reins coloured a deep magenta. The carriage body was very wide and on each side were glass windows that were changed for gauze in summertime. In the wintertime, the cover was lined inside with squirrel furs. Madame Tao sat inside the carriage, and at either side of her on the running boards were a coachman and a footman. In front, sitting cross-legged on the shaft was a maidservant carrying Madame Tao's silver water-pipe, which she was responsible for lighting. Following the carriage was an escort of a dozen or so horsemen and men on foot.

I heard that when my father travelled outside the Mansion, his entourage was even more extravagant. On *Qingming* (Clear and Bright) Festival[1] when he went to the Forest of Confucius to sweep the ancestral graves, the party consisted of one firecracker handler, four men with gongs, four with drums, four tall-hatted officials, two men at the carriage door carrying censers, two personal servants from the Inner Apartments carrying censers, three grooms, four coachmen, eight sedan-chair bearers, one relief sedan bearer, two sedan-chair assistants, four major footmen and five minor footmen, one regular attendant, fifteen family servants, numerous ceremonial guardsmen, two men from the Worship the Shadows Hall, minor servants from the Temple of Confucius, a cushion bearer, a man carrying sacrificial offerings, two with tea, two with silver, and one kitchen boy, totalling close to a hundred men. The procession created a great stir throughout the town as it passed to the clamour of gongs and drums. Whenever grandfather or great-grandfather made a trip to Beijing, not only were the numbers of ceremonial

[1] The *Qingming* Festival falls on the fiftieth day of the third month in the lunar calendar (usually early April). It used to be a great Buddhist festival but it is now absorbed into popular religion and families go out to their graves, sweep and weed them, offer food and burn paper money for the dead, to keep their souls comfortable.

guardsmen increased, but each town and county along the route had to prepare in advance: one seal keeper, one large sedan chair, three sets of chair bearers, eighteen *yamen* runners, thirty carriers, two saddle horses, twenty-five spare horses, ten grooms, ten mounted police, a band, complete wet-weather equipment in case of rain, and lanterns for use at night.

When my father went to Beijing, there was no need to notify towns along the way, for he could travel in first class comfort on the special direct train to the capital. It was only when my father's coffin was being transported back to Qufu that the Beijing Ministry of Internal Affairs directed local officials along the way to receive and see off the bier.

We children seldom left home. When we did, however, our guard of honour was smaller than Madame Tao's and our carriages (known as small secondary carriages) were less exquisite than hers. A third kind of carriage (called a large secondary carriage) slightly less splendid than ours was provided for the special use of Kong Mansion maidservants. Mansion runners generally travelled on horses raised in the Kong Mansion stables. When my brother was about ten years old, he travelled without a guard of honour, accompanied by three *yamen* runners and sometimes by a few security guards. We always left through the back gate and were not required to go through any ostentatious ceremonies.

Once when my elder sister was small, she went to Beijing on a pleasure outing and took a great fancy to the horse carriages she saw in the streets of the capital. She bought a carriage and horses and brought them back to Qufu along with a carriage driver named Feng. This became the first horse-drawn carriage in Qufu. The Kong Mansion subsequently replaced all its mule carriages with horse carriages which, at the time, were considered to be the height of fashion.

Because access to the Inner Apartments was severely restricted, and because on those rare occasions when we did go out it was in the midst of a noisy thronging crowd, most people felt there was something mysterious about life in the inner courtyards. When members of our own clan were chatting they also talked of life in the Inner Apartments as if it were an enigma. But in fact life there was not mysterious at all – just one woman and three small children living out their dull and uneventful lives.

The Kong Mansion was both the mansion of a duke and the home of the sage, so our everyday life was a mixture of the luxury of the aristocracy and the self-styled frugality of the scholar. The whole building complex was a typical mandarin's manor, permeated with the atmosphere of a literary family: inside and outside, on door frames and pillars hung such paired couplets as: 'There is no learning under heaven greater than that of Confucius,' 'The worthies of all eras have emanated from within these walls,' 'Ten thousand volumes of poetry and prose are at once comprehensible,' 'Long cultivated virtue shines with eternal brightness,' 'Choose friends carefully and in dealings with the world observe the rites,' 'Manage the household frugally, and in executing all duties be diligent.' On a screen wall in the Qiantang Building courtyard was a huge mural depicting '*Tan* eating the sun' (*Tan*, meaning 'greedy', was an insatiably greedy animal). The creature was treading gold and silver beneath his feet, but still looking at the sun with open jaws. I guess the ancestor who left this behind was seeking to use the hideous image to warn his descendants.

Generation after generation had lived here following the set routine, rarely implementing any changes. Life in the Inner Apartments was virtually cut off from the outside world, ultra-conservative and endlessly monotonous.

The Kong Mansion had an ancient tradition of making use of objects which had been handed down from ages past. Old household articles could not be casually discarded and unless it was absolutely necessary, no new article could be added. In the Hall of Loyalty and Forbearance, for example, there were over 130 objects such as gold-plated flower-pots, ancient bronze pitchers, jade flower-baskets, small bronze cooking-vessels (*ding*), an ancient bronze dressing-mirror, a phoenix mirror ornamented with king-fisher feathers, a jade mirror, a Chinese clock, jade-slab bells, a small square marble table, a sandalwood writing-brush container, a palace lantern with six ridges, a bamboo-root lion, a *qin* table, an Arhat bed, a gold censer, jade bowls, red-glazed porcelain bottles, imperial calligraphy, a miniature pavilion of treasures, a flat Han-dynasty vase, a hardwood inscribed footstool, coral plates, cloisonné cooking pots, collections of poetry of various emperors, historical works with emperors' handwritten annotations, maps of touring lodges, calligraphy models of eight great calligraphers, and landscape paintings. All these things had been in the room for generations and no article, large or small, could be rearranged at will, nor could additional articles be placed in the room.

But in line with the social progress that was made after the founding of the Republic, changes began to appear at the Kong Mansion. Glass dressing-mirrors were bought for the bedrooms. To anyone outside the Mansion, a glass mirror was quite a commonplace object, but for Mansion residents, using a glass mirror instead of the traditional bronze mirror was a marvellous innovation.

There were no thermos flasks, extremely common throughout China, in daily use at the Mansion. Although they were readily available in the town, no one even thought of buying one. If we wanted boiling water, we had to draw it from the 'tea brazier'. This was an unusual bronze contraption shaped like a huge chafing-dish. Wood or charcoal was burnt in the centre and water heated around it. Every time we went to the Forest of Confucius or on some other excursion, it would be brought along on a carrying pole, with the brazier hanging from one end and the fuel balancing it on the other. Compared with simply carrying a thermos of hot water, this was indeed a cumbersome custom.

Another example of rigid adherence to the old ways concerns the sedan-chair bearers. Even though sedan chairs had been dispensed with for everyday use long ago, and the bearers assigned other work, when lists of servants were drawn up, chair bearers were still included. When Decheng married, he was sent a car and chauffeur from Qingdao, but one official sedan-chair bearer was still employed at the Mansion. Since there was no chair for him to bear, he did odd jobs, but still listed his profession as chair bearer.

The Kong Mansion was famous throughout China for its traditional 'Lu' embroidery. Single and double thread embroidery, patchwork, and petit point were used to embroider purses, belts, boxes, coverlets, and hangings with landscapes, figures, flowers and plants, birds and animals, grasses and insects. There was a needle-woman at the Mansion named Zhu Erni whose embroidery was often given by the Kong Mansion as gifts. Her work was so exquisite that examples of it were framed and hung as pictures. There were also silkworm breeders and silk producers, one of whom, Tao Rong, was our frequent companion. We often went to the Houtang Building, where silk was made and stored, to watch him raising silkworms.

Although the Kong Mansion wove its own silk and produced its own embroidery, there was no sign of it in my own or my sister's bedrooms. In order to preserve the lifestyle of the descendants of a sage, we strictly observed our ancestors' exhortations to live simply and frugally. Our beds were covered with home-made handwoven sheets with print patterns of white flowers on a blue background (such as I found later were used in most country homes); and our quilts were made not of silk, but of ordinary patterned cotton. Our rooms were not decorated with the bright colours that young girls are so fond of, and the curtains and drapes were for the most part of an unembroidered, plain blue fabric.

Our clothing reflected the contradiction in lifestyles that I mentioned earlier. On the one hand, we had huge wardrobes of costly clothes, but on the other, they all remained locked away and we never wore them. Madame Tao, for example, had 162 articles of clothing made for her at one time in September 1916. There were over ten sable, squirrel and other valuable fur coats, as well as rich silks and satins. My father also had a huge wardrobe. His 'Notebook for Locating Clothes' records that in one year he had over 400 major articles of clothing made.

We, of course, had many clothes too, but we had never set eyes on most of them. Unbelievable as it may seem, we two 'young ladies' went about in outfits identical to those of any other ordinary girls. We wore blue cotton gowns, and black cloth shoes. This was to signify that we lived the frugal lives of descendants of the sage! Because Decheng was a boy he dressed even more simply. Only at festivals and special celebrations did we dress up in silks and satins, adorn ourselves with flowers and put on a little rouge.

My sister and I had a typical young girl's desire for beauty, and were not satisfied with wearing blue gowns and black cloth shoes. But we had no idea of what went on in the outside world or of conventional beauty. We rarely left the Kong Mansion, and there were even places in the Kong Mansion that we never visited. Thus we had no idea of fashion at all. Take shoes for instance. Apart from home-made cloth shoes, we knew no other forms of footwear. When I was about ten, a relative sent my sister and me a pair of galoshes, shiny and black with low-cut sides. Only then they weren't

known as 'rainshoes' and the person who sent them had no idea
they were supposed to be worn in the rain. Pointing to the shine on
the black rubber, he told us there was light in the shoes and that they
were currently the most fashionable thing in the big city. This was
the first and only time before we were married that we set eyes on
anything other than cloth shoes. How we treasured them! We didn't
know what they were made of, but the 'light' on the surface amazed
us. Although it was the height of summer, the two of us paraded
around the Kong Mansion in our rubber shoes as if we were
strolling down the main street. When we met someone and showed
them our new shoes, they would invariably answer:

'Tut-tut! Times are really changing. Young ladies wear shoes
with lights now!' But whether this was meant as praise or derision
I'm not sure.

Later my sister and I became even more 'chic'. We were given
knitted (foreign) socks from Beijing and Jinan, but had no idea how
to wear them, so we just guessed. First we put on our home-made
white cloth socks and wore the new socks over them. Despite the
fact that this was extremely hot and uncomfortable, we were
exceedingly pleased with ourselves. Only being interested in
looking beautiful, we were happy to endure the stifling heat.

We wore the round, flat, black velveteen hats traditionally worn
in the countryside by old women. We were under the impression
that women of all ages wore hats like these and never thought to ask
if hats came in any other styles. To add a little decoration, we picked
out pearls and pieces of jadeite and sewed them around the brims.

As small children, we wore our hair in a single long plait down
our backs tied with red ribbon. But at the age of ten or so we learned
how to coil our hair high on our heads. Despite the fact that the
Republic had been proclaimed many years before, we were still
doing our hair in the style of Manchu women of the early Qing
dynasty.

We had no particular liking for silks and satins and the most
fashionable clothes that Deqi and I had before we were married
were patterned gowns from Jinan. Unlike us, Decheng had no desire
to follow fashion and simply wore what was made for him. From
the age of two or three until he was married, he wore a long gown,
mandarin jacket and small hat sewn with pearls in the form of the
character 'Longevity'.

My Childhood

People often talk of the 'golden years of their childhood', but what 'colour' were my early years? They seem to have been covered in a layer of dust. Yet beneath the dust lay the soft, tender heart of a child, sincere feelings and innocent, unadulterated laughter and dreams.

All children have friends, classmates, neighbours and relatives, but we had none. In that huge house there were only three small children. We always did everything together and never once quarrelled. If we were playing and my little brother was called away to meet guests, we would stop and wait for him to come back. Eating, sleeping, reading and playing -- we were never apart from dawn till dusk.

Decheng was the 'little duke', the 'little sage', so naturally he was treated differently from my sister and myself. For example, at the Dragon Boat Festival, a solution of red orpiment would be daubed on our foreheads to ward off evil during the coming year. Decheng would have the character 'wang' (king) daubed on his forehead while my sister and I had a few horizontal lines.

Besides this, stories grew up around Decheng as they had around each Yansheng Duke throughout history. For example, it was said that a giant snake once coiled itself up on top of one of the doors. People tried to shut the door but found it impossible to move. At last one of the errand boys climbed up to take a look, but, struck with terror, fell back in a faint. The door remained open. Fortunately just then my brother came in. Just as he was entering the doorway, the snake fled . . . and so the stories go – too numerous to mention. Many of the incidents they relate are unknown to even Decheng himself.

While the three of us were together, especially when we were playing, Decheng always went along with our suggestions. Hide and seek, playing house, catch . . . whatever Deqi and I decided to do, he would do too. We had very few playmates. One of them was a little boy called Liu Sanyuan whose old grandfather served as our doctor. On visits to the Mansion, the old man would bring Liu Sanyuan along to 'act as his walking stick'. When Sanyuan's grandfather died, his father took over his duties and continued to bring the little boy with him. Even when no one was ill, we would send messages to his house and invite him to come and play. When he grew a little older, he came to the Mansion and worked as a clerk in the library, where he became a skilful calligrapher and learned to recite many of the classics. He also learned medicine from his father.

Besides Liu Sanyuan, there was the daughter of Decheng's wet nurse Mother Zhang, whom we all called Mama Ni. When she wasn't working, she would often come and play with us. Later she left the Kong Mansion to help her father in the fields, but still frequently came back to see us. Other friends were Little Zhu Xiao and Zhu Erni. We spent many merry hours together without distinguishing between master and servant, between 'respected' and 'lowly'. We had a little flat wooden cart pulled by a pair of black and white goats. My sister and I and Liu Sanyuan used to sit on the cart while Decheng, whip in hand, ran alongside urging the animals on.

When we were small, we had no toys because our ancestors had not bequeathed any to us, and as mentioned above, the Kong Mansion didn't buy anything new. All we had to play with were pearls and kingfisher feathers, agate and gold. Apart from that, the Inner Apartments were full of rubbings of pictures of the sage and stone inscriptions that we used to fold up into playthings. When we played 'house' we had no rag doll, but used instead dried millet stalks from the Rear Flower Garden that we tied up into makeshift dolls. Later when one of the servants made us the little cart and brought us the two goats, this became the only toy of our childhood years.

We often played in the Rear Flower Garden in a cave in the rockery which we called our 'old nest'. There we chased and sported around, without considering the question of whether my little brother was a sage or not. Once Decheng threw a lump of earth at Liu Sanyuan, who began to cry. Decheng got very worried and quickly ran over to console him, then ran off and got some ointment for his bruise and begged him not to tell Madame Tao. Another time when Liu Sanyuan was visiting us, we played a juggling game called 'Three Spirits Pass the Cover'. My brother put a glass marble in his mouth and in a moment of excitement swallowed it. Liu Sanyuan was scared out of his wits and the entire Kong Mansion was greatly alarmed. No one could relax until Decheng eliminated the marble during a routine defecation.

Madame Tao didn't like to see us playing and hated the sight of us running and laughing. She would scold: 'Just calm down a bit!' but in fact, our grandmother disliked *her* because of her lack of poise. After she and my father were married, my grandmother criticised her for always walking around in a fluster – not in the least dignified or sedate and quite lacking the bearing of a Lady of the First Rank. When we played we always kept a wary eye out for Madame Tao. If we saw her coming we would stop playing and wait until she had walked away before resuming our game.

Inside the wall of the Eastern College that divided the Kong Mansion from the street outside, there was a pile of earth high enough to allow us to see over the top of the wall. Sometimes when we were feeling bored, we would climb the earth pile and cling to the top of the wall, watching the passers-by, stallkeepers and pedlars, and examining the shop-fronts. Later the servants decided that this was too unrefined for the duke and his sisters, if not downright improper. But since it could not easily be stopped, they worked out a solution: atop the pile of earth they built a small platform over which they erected a canopy; that way we could sit 'in state' and comfortably watch the world beyond the walls.

From birth to marriage, I lived in the Kong Mansion for seventeen years. In those years I never once went to a regular theatre and had no idea what a movie was. We attended opera performances in the courtyard of the Qianshang Building. When putting up the stage in the courtyard, workmen were not permitted to dig holes for the supporting pillars, since disturbing the soil at random might destroy the *fengshui*[1] of the Kong Mansion. Four huge blocks of stone with sockets drilled into them were kept in the courtyard especially for holding up the supports. I always found it strange that although it was not permissible to dig holes for the stage supports, no one took any notice when my brother's wet nurse, Mother Zhang, pulled up grey paving stones in the Qiantang Building Courtyard and planted a large patch of melons. Even Madame Tao pretended not to notice anything – probably because of her personal connections with the wet nurse.

To return to the stage – opera was the only amusement that the

[1] *Fengshui*, or geomancy: the location of a house or tomb in relation to the local geographical features, supposed to influence the family's fortune.

Kong Mansion ever indulged in.[1] My father was an opera fan and at the end of the Qing dynasty permanently engaged two theatre troupes; a Beijing troupe and a Shandong troupe. Each had complete sets of costumes and props, and performers from Beijing and Jinan resided in the Mansion. The troupes were later disbanded, but some of the members stayed on at the Mansion as stewards. The chests of costumes and properties were also kept and each time an opera was staged, these old actors would perform for us, assisted by other servants, such as Chen Xinquan, the ostler who played 'painted face' roles,[2] and the gardener Lao Chen who played bit roles. Their performances were not of a high standard but the costumes were exquisite enough to hold one entranced. Furthermore, I had never seen a professional opera troupe so I had nothing to compare them with.

Besides enjoying operas, we often performed our own operas, and asked Sanyuan, Mama Ni and sometimes my brother's steward, Chen Jingrong, to join in. In the Houtang Building we would don costumes made from odds and ends of silks and satins, while the silkworm breeder, Tao Rong, stood guard for us. If he saw Madame Tao coming, he would clap his hands and we would immediately stop and wait until she had passed by. Decheng couldn't bear the waiting and would impatiently ask: 'Where did we get up to just now?' Whereupon we would resume our singing. We sang 'The Capture and Release of Caocao', 'Lu Wenlong Views the Pictures', among others. Once an opera was staged at the Kong Mansion in which my brother took part. His special role was to seize a 'lion', but he was too impatient and went after it before his cue. Everyone teased him about it when the performance was over.

[1] Beijing opera is a mainly Qing dynasty development from earlier forms of drama and in its characteristic form is more than an opera, for it comprises spoken parts, singing, dancing and acrobatics. The stories are mainly based on heroic historic or legendary figures, male or female, although all female parts were traditionally taken by male actors.

[2] All actors in Beijing opera or the local forms wore make-up but that for those playing heroic or female roles was reasonably naturalistic. Painted face make-up is highly stylised, with brightly coloured stripes and circles. The colours and the forms of the patterns indicate the type of character: a black face with white eyebrows indicates uprightness and morality; a pale face with a black line down the nose and across the cheeks denotes loyalty and a strong temperament, whilst a completely white face indicates untrustworthiness, and so on.

After playing for a while, we would get hungry and send someone to the kitchen with a bamboo basket to fetch steamed bread or cakes. When it arrived, my brother or I would divide it into equal portions according to the number of people present. Sometimes someone would bring steamed bread from home and Decheng would always ask for a share of that too.

We very rarely ate food from outside the Mansion, but sometimes we'd send a servant to locate Zhao Beng'er, a Qufu pedlar with a shoulder pole full of snacks and sweets. He would come to the Mansion with trays piled high with peanut toffee, candied crab-apples, crab-apple jelly and other confections. We would call together all the servants we could find, and would all stand around his shoulder pole eating whatever took our fancy. We always felt that things from outside were much fresher and more delicious than anything we had at home. When the trays had been completely emptied, we would send Zhao Beng'er to the accountant to collect his payment.

When we fell ill, a sedan chair would be sent to bring old Doctor Liu to the Inner Apartments. Liu Jinpei's ancestors had been skilled doctors for many generations. In my grandfather's day, Dr Liu had been appointed to the Kong Mansion by the emperor, but afterwards had somehow offended Madame Tao and been forced to leave. Later my father fell ill, and several other doctors who were called in were unable to effect a cure. Finally Dr Liu was asked to treat him. After taking a single dose of medicine, father's illness took a turn for the better. After three doses, he completely recovered. From then on, if anyone was ill we took whatever Dr Liu prescribed. But having once thrown him out of the Mansion, Madame Tao could not invite him back, so each time he was needed, a sedan chair would be sent out to fetch him.

When Liu Jinpei died, his son Liu Mengying became our physician. Liu Mengying was extremely loyal to the Kong Mansion and besides his regular duties, often helped my father with business affairs. Sometimes father would keep sums of money at his house and forget all about it, but years later Liu would remind him of it. Once Liu arranged for the Kong Mansion to lend money to a man who subsequently went bankrupt. Liu Mengying didn't say a word to my father, but privately sold some of his property, borrowed some money and returned the debt.

Once when Decheng fell seriously ill, Liu Mengying sat by his bed night and day. Dr Liu kept a strong decoction of opium at home and had made all the arrangements for his own funeral. He said to his wife: 'The moment the young duke dies, I shall take that opium.' Only after Decheng recovered did we learn about this vow. We trusted him implicitly, for he was a highly skilled physician. He set the written exams for medical students in Qufu and also conducted their practical examinations. Later, his son Liu Sanyuan also studied medicine and many of the citizens of Qufu consulted him when they were ill.

We occasionally went on pleasure outings to the Kong Mansion villa at Pan Lake. My father had built the villa in a beautiful scenic area of ponds and mountains. The shrimps in the lake were exceptionally transparent, and when I asked one of the maidservants about this, she replied that it was because the emperor had set his eyes upon them once. She also explained that the frogs in Pan Lake didn't croak because when the emperor lived here he had become irritated by the continual noise, and issued an order that the frogs should not croak any more.

Apart from those trips, we sometimes played in the Xiguan Flower Garden. My brother still has a photograph of himself taken there. He was seven or eight at the time, and the picture shows him standing between two enormous, heavily-armed security guards specially assigned to protect him.

My Wet Nurse

I cherish fond memories of my wet nurse, Mother Wang. A few months after I was born she began to feed and raise me, and from then on I lived under her constant care. Throughout my childhood she occupied a place in my heart that Madame Tao could never have rivalled.

In our relationships with Madame Tao it was impossible to talk of any tender feelings between mother and daughter or mother and son. Everything was regulated by the Confucian rites and family rules, and there was no emotion involved. But my wet nurse, Mother Wang, was a real person who was kindly, gentle and sincere. From this country woman, I received the maternal love and warmth that I never could have known with Madame Tao.

I was the apple of her eye and she loved me to the day she died. I remember how each morning after she had finished combing my hair, washing and dressing me, she would smile in delight as if admiring her own masterpiece. Sometimes she would mutter to herself: 'So much the image of her own mother!' These were words of praise, and as she spoke her eyes would fill with gratification and a little sadness.

I could play and laugh before her to my heart's content and she never admonished me as Madame Tao used to. She would say: 'Show me a child who doesn't live to play!' She had an inexhaustible store of ancient legends that filled my head with innumerable magical fantasies.

She was warm and sincere to everyone around her and displayed a spirit of self-sacrifice that I shall never forget. I remember when she fell ill once and was just about to take her medicine when she heard that an errand runner was also ill and needed this kind of medicine but was unable to buy it. She immediately sent him all of her own medicine. Several years later Liu Sanyuan was greatly moved when he recalled this incident, but to Mother Wang it was nothing out of the ordinary.

After I married and moved to Beijing, she accompanied me to the capital, and shed many secret tears when she realised my married life was so unhappy. In trying to protect my just rights (when my husband demanded my money and property or when he treated me roughly) she displayed a staunchness that she had never shown in all her years at the Kong Mansion. As a descendant of the sage who had been brought up in a scholar's study, I had always been taught to treat people according to the rites and had no idea how to cope with people in the real world who did not always behave according to the dictates of propriety, but Mother Wang always argued strongly for my fair treatment without showing the slightest fear. But as our marital contradictions became more and more acute and I found myself at a total loss concerning how to solve the problem, Mother Wang returned to Qufu alone, in order to spare me any further embarrassment. But her heart was always with me. Later, when she learned that I was in straitened circumstances, she sent me money and a hand-made padded jacket, trousers and shoes. It was the depths of winter, so it was really a case of 'delivering charcoal in the snow'; the clothes were all of silk and satin, exquisitely made. At that time, Mother Wang was a lonely old woman living in the remote countryside in very difficult circumstances herself. How did she manage to make me such costly padded clothes, and what hunger and cold did she endure in order to send such warmth to her distant nurseling?

In 1979, when I was over sixty, I had the chance to return to Qufu, and my greatest wish was to see my beloved Mother Wang. But she had already left this world. My brother's wet nurse, Mother Zhang, had also died of illness, but her daughter Mama Ni was still alive. Decheng's wet nurse was a rather special case, since she was not one of the Kong Mansion hereditary servants. There's an interesting story attached to her employment at the Mansion.

When my brother was born, he cried loudly without ceasing. Ten different wet nurses were hired, but none of them was suitable. Some of them couldn't supply enough milk, while others made his stomach upset – everyone in the Kong Mansion was very anxious. Then Liu Mengying discovered a young beggar woman sitting at the main gate of the Temple of Confucius with her baby daughter in her arms. Her clothes were in rags, but the tiny girl was extremely plump. The woman was brought into the Mansion, bathed, and given clean clothes, and after finishing off a huge bowl of sea-cucumber soup fed Decheng. Decheng fed hungrily and went peacefully to sleep. Madame Tao was very satisfied and put her on a three-day trial. Everyone said it was the 'will of heaven' that she should have been found at the gate of the Temple of Confucius, and she and her daughter were thereupon taken on at the Mansion. Mother Zhang's food was specially prepared in a small kitchen: every morning a leg of pork was stewed for her and every evening a chicken. Each day she was given one and a quarter kilos of steamed bread. Her daughter was sent home to be cared for by her mother-in-law who received a daily ration of a half kilo of steamed bread and almost a quarter kilo of white sugar. Her husband was given over an acre and a half of land and a house was built so the family could settle in Qufu. After my brother was weaned at the age of nine months, Mother Zhang stayed on at the Mansion and continued to live there for over thirty years.

We three children all lived with Madame Tao in the eastern

section of the Qiantang Building. My elder sister and I each had a bed in the inner room and my brother and Madame Tao shared a bed in the outer room. Mother Zhang slept alone on a little cot in the middle of the room. She always slept fully dressed so that she could get up immediately whenever she was called.

Mother Zhang adored her nurseling Decheng. She fell seriously ill during the ten years of turmoil that engulfed China at the time of the 'cultural revolution' and as she lay dying cried over and over again, 'Little Cheng is on his way . . . Little Cheng will be here!' To the hour of her death she still cherished the memory of her nurseling far away in Taiwan.

The wet nurses were allowed to use our pet names just as Madame Tao did. They called my elder sister 'Number-One Sister', me 'Number-Two Sister', and my brother 'Little Cheng'. Everyone else had to call us 'Elder Miss', 'Second Miss' and 'Little Duke'. Besides our wet nurses, there was a manservant named Chen Jingrong whose special task was to care for us. When I was small, he used to carry me around all day and afterwards was charged with the care of Decheng. He, Wu Jianzhang and Li Fengming all shared this task, and were constantly at his side. In the summertime, each time my brother slept alone, Li Fengming would lower the mosquito netting and fan him for a long time from outside the net. During Decheng's childhood, Chen and Wu took care of him when he conducted sacrifices to Confucius. In 1937 Chen and Wu followed my brother to Chongqing and then to Nanjing. In late 1949, they went with him to Taiwan. While in Nanjing, Chen Jingrong accompanied Decheng whenever he left home, handling all the daily expenses on his behalf.

My elder sister's wet nurse was also named Wang; so as to differentiate her from my Mother Wang, everyone called her Elder Mother Wang. When my elder sister married she didn't accompany her to her new home.

The Family School

When we reached the age of five, we three children began to attend classes at the family school. At first, the classroom was in the west room of the Qianshang Building, but later it was shifted to a room to the rear of the Western College. Outside the classroom door hung a pair of paired couplets engraved on wood panels. The right-hand inscription read: 'To the east is the family compound; we study the *Book of Odes* and the rites to restore the ancestral ways.' The left hand inscription read: 'To the west is the ancestral temple; we study with the ancestral ideals in view.' In the centre of the room was a table dedicated to Confucius and a large desk used by the teacher. Before the window were our three small desks and chairs and some flower-pots. A large clock hung on the wall. Our teaching staff consisted of Teacher Lü, Teacher Wang and a succession of short-term teachers: Zhan, Bian and Zhuang.

The curriculum was largely made up of the Four Books, (the sacred canon of Confucianism – *The Doctrine of the Mean*, *The Great Learning*, *The Analects of Confucius* and *Mencius*)[1] and the Five Classics (*The Book of Odes*, *The Book of History*, *The Book of Changes*, *The Book of Rites* and *The Spring and Autumn Annals*), as well as music (playing the seven string *qin*), mathematics and English. Later geography and history were added. The latter four 'modern' subjects reveal the influence of the times. Apart from these classes, we spent hours each day practising writing. The Kong Mansion was fastidious about teaching calligraphy. When visitors came to the Mansion, the 'four treasures of the scholar's studio' – brushes, ink, inkslab and paper – would be laid out on the long table in the Qianshang Building and guest and host would exchange scrolls of their work. This became part of the protocol that could not be neglected when important guests were received. When Decheng reached the age of seven, people began to make requests for his calligraphy, and as he grew older these requests increased. In fact, he had so many requests that I frequently wrote on his behalf. When I returned to Qufu last year I saw some of my father's and Decheng's calligraphy on sale in the antique shop, and I heard that paired couplets I wrote as a child are still preserved in the storerooms.

Thinking back, I realise that our student life was exceptionally dry and insipid. We worked very hard all day with little time set aside for recreation. We only had one official rest day in ten, but in

[1]The Four Books are four short texts with commentaries by Zhu Xi (see p. 112), and they include the Analects or sayings of Confucius himself and anecdotes illustrating his views, and the *Mencius*, the collected views of his most famous early follower (see p. 17).

fact we never rested. Our teachers strictly controlled our study timetable, and if guests came to visit my brother, the teacher would limit the time they could spend together and demand that Decheng return promptly to his studies. Even after classes were over, guests could only be received with the teacher's consent.

When we rose each morning, we were washed and dressed by our wet nurses and then shuffled straight to the classroom for the first lesson of the day. We studied until eight o'clock and then ate breakfast in the classroom with our teacher. After the meal we would continue studying until lunchtime, when we would return to the Inner Apartments and eat with Madame Tao. After lunch, it was back to the classroom until five or six o'clock, when we would return for the evening meal. In winter, dinner would be followed by a session of 'lantern study' in the classroom, after which we would go straight to bed. In the summer there was no lantern study, and we sat in the coolness of the Rear Flower Garden. Generally we had no holidays, and only on the days when sacrifices to Confucius were held or when we had to sweep the graves were there no classes. Apart from that we had a few days off at New Year.

The day on which classes started after the New Year was determined by the teacher in accordance with the almanac. On the first day of school, Confucius' tablet was placed on a desk in the classroom. We would first kowtow to the tablet and the teacher, then begin a new year of study. The teacher rarely explained the texts we read. Since we were only required to learn them by heart – not only in the correct sentence order, but backwards as well – we had no idea of the meaning of what we recited. At our first class, the teacher made us recite a poem from *The Book of Odes*: 'The water birds cry from an isle in the river. Beautiful maiden chaste and serene, perfect match for the gentleman!' Having recited it forwards, we then had to recite it backwards: 'Perfect match for the gentleman, beautiful maiden chaste and serene. From an isle in the river the water birds cry.' Once I mastered this, the teacher smiled and nodded his head, but gave no explanation. After class I asked somebody what 'Beautiful maiden chaste and serene, perfect match for the gentleman!' meant and received the reply: 'My dear child, why ask?' So from then on, I learned to recite without asking questions.

We were very young to be studying from morning till night, but although we recited texts until our heads whirled, we were never impatient to play and actually worked quite hard. Outside the schoolroom stood a huge white pomegranate tree that filled with a mass of tiny white blossoms in summer. The heady scent floated in through the windows, impelling us to lay down our books and play under its branches. But without waiting to be called, the three of us would return to the classroom together and continue our work.

While we were studying, Madame Tao occasionally came to watch. She seemed to be carrying out an inspection, but never asked any questions. She just stood there for a while and left. Perhaps this had something to do with etiquette!

While we were at classes, our other teachers rested in their rooms, read or practised calligraphy. These teachers had only been engaged following lengthy deliberations between Madame Tao and the rest of the family. The first to be thus engaged was Teacher Wang Yuhua from Laiwu County. He was a graduate of one of the new style academies, so his basic grounding in the classics was relatively weak. Not long after his arrival at the Mansion some family members raised objections, saying that if we studied under graduates of the new academies, future descendants of the sage would soon forget their ancestral origins. By happy coincidence, Zhuang Hailan visited the Mansion at this time as a member of the Chinese Postal Service delegation. Zhuang was almost seventy and a former scholar of the Imperial Academy, with notable attainments in the fields of calligraphy and the classics. The family prevailed on him to stay on as a teacher and he finally agreed on the condition that he receive no salary but live at the Mansion as a guest. He taught us the classics and the study of rhyme.

Later Teacher Zhuang brought in another teacher, Lü Jinshan, to assist him at the Mansion. Teacher Lü had been a successful candidate in the imperial provincial examinations and was a few years younger than his colleague. From then on, Teacher Wang seldom taught classes and generally just coached us individually.

The three teachers became 'loyal subjects' of the Kong Mansion. They lived at the Mansion all year round, seldom visiting their own homes. When I was eleven, Madame Tao developed hemiplegia and Decheng, who had originally slept alongside her, moved into Teacher Wang's room. Teacher Wang took great care of him and would often get up in the night to rearrange his quilt for him.

Whenever Teacher Lü's wife made her occasional visits to the Mansion, Teacher Lü would invite us all to a meal, and in summer would often take the three of us for a stroll in the garden after classes. Apart from solving study problems, Teacher Lü also instructed my brother on questions of social interaction with relatives, friends and officials. When banquets were held for important guests, the teachers were always invited to attend.

On the eve of the Anti-Japanese War, when Decheng left Qufu for Chongqing accompanied by Teacher Lü, Teacher Wang remained at the Mansion to help run Mansion affairs. Although Teacher Zhuang was quite an old man he also remained at Qufu and continued to teach us. After the war ended in 1945, Decheng moved from Chongqing to Nanjing and Teacher Wang joined him. Wang and Lü both lived over the Kong Decheng Administration Office and in 1949 accompanied Decheng to Taiwan.

Teacher Wang was a very liberal-minded man, vigorously opposed to the binding of women's feet. By coincidence, he arrived at the Mansion just a few days after my elder sister's feet were bound for the first time. She was in great distress, sobbing all day long, so Teacher Wang firmly insisted that the bandages be taken off. Teacher Lü did not oppose him. The Kong Mansion had a great respect for its teachers and generally followed their suggestions, so Deqi's feet were unbound. As a result I never had my feet bound at all, and we became the first generation of Kong Mansion women to have 'big feet'.

When we started school, Teacher Wang asked us to keep a diary and write a poem in it every day. The following were written by Decheng around the age of ten:

Studying at Night
The little thatched study is cold tonight,
By the icy light of a single lantern,
I spend the hours reciting poetry.
A dog's howl sounds clear through the stillness
of the deep alleys.
To the sound of my chanting, the moon rises.

Red Leaves
Where are autumn trees like the maples of Jiangnan

Adorning the garden with a crimson belt?
Like the fresh blood of soldiers shed in battle,
Sprinkled at random through the forest.

Our teachers seldom praised our writing and generally only pointed out our faults, but always gently. If they discovered a sentence in our exercises they liked, they would read it over and over again. I remember that when Teacher Zhuang read my brother's lines: 'In the maple forests the first red leaves appear, homing rooks, black against the sky, bespeak an infinite melancholy', he was overjoyed and, with a smile on his face, read it to himself several times. But he didn't praise it, he said: 'You must still improve the style and tone of your poetry, it mustn't be so depressing!'

We also learned arithmetic, and when I think of it now, it seems quite ridiculous: whether writing horizontally or vertically, we always used writing brushes and never owned either a pencil or a fountain pen. The solutions had to be written under each problem with meticulous care in tiny brushstrokes.

We frequently had examinations of all kinds. Apart from having to write poetry and essays, we had to answer questions, fill in blanks, write passages from memory, and correct improperly written characters. Our results almost always hovered around 90 per cent, but we seldom got perfect marks. All exam results were taken by the schoolroom attendant and reported to Madame Tao. Whenever family elders came to visit the Mansion, they would always ask to know the results of our most recent examinations.

On every homework exercise or exam paper, we were required to write our age, name and style. My sister Deqi's style was Boping; mine was Zhongshu; and my little brother's Dasheng. When he was nine, he wrote on each paper: 'Nine years old; Kong Decheng; Dasheng; seventy-seventh generation grandson.'[1]

Wu Jianzhang and Chen Jingrong accompanied us to school every day and waited in an adjacent room while we attended lessons. They kept a continuous watch and as soon as we came out

[1] Deqi's 'style' or literary name and that of Demao are complex for they include two separate concepts: in each, the first character refers to their relative seniority within the family and the second character, unrelated to the first, is that of a quality. Deqi's style means 'eldest' and 'peace'; Demao's 'second' and 'kindness'. Decheng's is more straightforward and means 'distinguished birth'.

of class they would escort us back home. There was also a footman called Wu Jianwen permanently assigned to work in the classroom. He was the brother of Wu Jianzhang and about ten years our senior. While we studied he would carefully attend us and always accompanied us home along with his brother and Chen Jingrong. In winter our lantern studies didn't end until eight or nine o'clock at night, when the buildings and courtyards of the Kong Mansion were pitch dark. Wu Jianwen, a small lantern in hand, led us along the long, winding corridors, repeatedly reminding us in gentle tones to mind the steps, or urging us not to be afraid. The scene left a very deep impression on me.

When my elder sister married into a Beijing family, Wu Jianwen accompanied her there as a footman. Deqi's married life was melancholy and joyless and she died a lonely death at the age of twenty-five. Her bier was placed in the Fayuan Temple in Beijing. Wu Jianwen wept bitterly at her death and maintained a long, solitary vigil beside her coffin. Afterwards, he continued to look after her two young sons until he died an old man.

Wu Jianwen's brother, Wu Jianzhang, followed Decheng to Chongqing, Nanjing and Taiwan. If he is still alive today, he must be over eighty years old.

The New Year Festival

The liveliest time of year was the lunar New Year Festival.

At the Kong Mansion, the sacrifice to the Kitchen God[1] was quite different from that held in other people's homes. In the latter, the Kitchen God was treated with pious respect, but in the Kong Mansion he was disdained. The family ranked the Kitchen God far below the Yansheng Duke and considered him inferior to the Duke in terms of both wealth and power, so the masters of the Kong

---

[1] In ordinary households, the Kitchen God commanded great respect. Each house had a shrine for him on the rear wall of the kitchen behind the hearth. On the 23rd day of the 12th lunar month, the Kitchen God made an annual trip to heaven to report on the conduct of the household. Offerings were placed before his portrait in a ceremony presided over by the head of the household and the portrait was sometimes smeared with honey or rice wine to ensure he would only say 'sweet' things when he got to heaven.

Mansion never personally sacrificed to him, leaving this to the servants.

The room in which the image of the Kitchen God was placed was dark and dismal. Since he was not considered worthy enough to receive sacrifices in one of the Kong Mansion kitchens his portrait was pasted up in a long-disused wood shed with blackened walls, full of soot and spiders' webs. But the ceremony was noisy and cheerful: there were always seven or eight drummers and buglers along with a cushion bearer and some footmen carrying sacrificial objects. During the sacrifice, the servant in charge would give directions to the god in a commanding tone, with no hint of pleading, for 'the sage has the protection of heaven' and the Kitchen God was powerless to influence heaven against him. But in our time no one paid much attention to these details; the main aim was to have fun, so my younger brother carried out the sacrifice in person, accompanied by Liu Sanyuan and a large crowd of servants.

On the eighth day of the twelfth lunar month (*Laba*) there came a complicated ritual of eating '*Laba* gruel'. Usually servants went home for their meals, but on this day, they all took their gruel at the Mansion. In addition, gruel was sent to all the members of the family in the Twelve Mansions and was offered to the ancestral tablets and the entire pantheon of deities. A large number of servants were assigned to prepare the gruel and the fire-tender family was called to the Mansion to keep the cooking fires burning. Huge pots were propped up over the flames and the gruel was ladled into several huge vats. There were two kinds of *Laba* gruel: a coarse version for the servants made from rice, slices of meat, cabbage and beancurd, which they ate with half a kilo of steamed bread per person; and a more refined kind for the Inner Apartments, Twelve Mansions and for offering to the ancestors. This was a special mixture of delicacies including the seeds of Job's tears, longans, lotus seeds, lily buds, chestnuts, dates, red beans and glutinous rice. On top of the gruel were placed intricately made decorations such as Chinese hawthorn-berries carved into tiny hollow baskets. We always saved these for last so that we could admire them for as long as possible.

Offering gruel to the ancestors and deities was an extremely finicky affair. The chapel alone contained hundreds of Buddhist and Daoist images: Guangong, the God of War; Yuhuang Dadi, the

Jade Emperor of Heaven; Guanyin, the Goddess of Mercy; the Amitabha Buddha; the Goddess of Childbearing . . . each deity had to have a bowl of gruel placed before it. After the time-consuming business of dishing it all out had been completed, it was put back in the pot and given to the chapel attendant. When I was ten, the attendant was a smart man named Chen who updated the method of presenting the offerings. He placed a huge dish of gruel in the centre of the chapel for the gods to eat from in common, and after a suitable period of time, took it home. I saw him offer sacrifices like this several times and thought it very novel and amusing. None of the ceremonial officers censured him for this innovation.

Monks and nuns from outside the Kong Mansion came to ask for gruel and their 'allotment' of rice. They lived in the local Dazhuang Temple, and Dongguan Goddess Temple and even Mount Tai. Before my brother was born, Madame Tao would send someone to Mount Tai every year on the eighth day of the first month to 'tether a baby' – a string was tied around the neck of a clay baby in the hope of getting a much-desired son. My father also visited Mount Tai and made vows to requite the kindness of the gods should they grant him a son. Thus everyone used to say that my little brother had been brought from Mount Tai on a tether, and as a result, after his birth representatives were sent to the mountain on his behalf to acknowledge the nuns there as his teachers. Servants were also sent there to burn incense in partial fulfilment of father's vow, and nuns came for rice before the New Year to receive their due share of alms.

Once *Laba* was passed, everyone busied themselves preparing for the New Year. Every room was cleaned, coloured marquees were erected, red carpets laid down, chair cushions changed and palace lanterns hung about. In every kitchen in the Mansion, three shifts of kitchen hands worked simultaneously steaming bread, meat dumplings and cakes. The fire-tender family also came to the Inner Apartments, working day and night to keep the fires burning. Barrels of steamed bread filled several large rooms. The steamed bread was made in many sizes and shapes, finely differentiated according to their designated purpose: there was bread for sacrificial offerings and for people to eat, for ordinary meals and for feasts. How we loved the happy, lively atmosphere filled with the sounds of laughter and chatter. In those days, the moment school was over we could rush back home and watch the cooks at work.

At that time of year we had our own tasks to perform. Every day we wrote numerous pairs of paired couplets, for at New Year, relatives and friends and all the Mansion servants requested calligraphy from Decheng. I gave my brother a hand, and we would write a dozen or so couplets each day. When the two of us couldn't keep up with the demand, one of the schoolmasters would also lend a hand.

When the steaming was finished every maidservant in the Inner Apartments was presented with a basket of steamed bread, steamed dumplings and New Year's cake. And on New Year's Eve, everyone gathered in the Inner Apartments and spent all night preparing boiled meat dumplings. The Mansion was festooned throughout with tasselled glass lanterns, ox-horn palace lanterns and tall, red candles. Sandalwood incense was burnt in bronze censers shaped like cranes, and rainbow streamers added to the festive atmosphere. After lunch we three children went to the Requite Ancestral Kindness Hall to pay our respects and after dinner saw out the old year at the Ancestral Temple and worshipped at the Requite Ancestral Kindness Hall. After this, we returned home and ran around playing until we were so tired that we fell asleep. At two or three o'clock we would be woken up to pay our respects to the God of Heaven and Earth, a formality unique to the Kong Mansion. In the courtyard of the Qianshang Building, a 'Heaven and Earth Tower' facing the eight points of the compass was built from straw mats. Inside were tables holding the tablets of the many gods and spirits, with the tablet of the God of Heaven and Earth occupying the central table. The positions of the remaining tablets changed each year in accordance with the almanac. We were roused from our beds half-asleep and facing each tablet in turn kowtowed endlessly before going back to bed.

Next to the Heaven and Earth Tower, a 'heaven-facing pole' was erected from which a 'heavenly lantern' was hung: this consisted of a long bamboo-pole stuck in the ground topped with a huge glass-lantern that was kept burning continuously for two weeks. The pole was so high that the lantern was visible throughout the town of Qufu.

On New Year's Eve, the adults would place money wrapped in

red paper written with the characters 'may you live a hundred years' beside our pillows, *ruyi*[1] (good luck symbols) made of sticky rice-flour, persimmons and oranges were put into our cloisonné food boxes. When we awoke next morning, we were not permitted to speak but could feel these things with our hands. Our first task in the morning was to worship at the Temple of Confucius and the Clan Hall.

I remember the first day of the lunar year as being devoted to nothing but kowtowing. Starting in the morning, all the servants of the Kong Mansion came to wish us a happy New Year – the one time they were allowed into the Inner Apartments. Madame Tao sat in an armchair in the main room of the Qianshang Building while my brother, sister and I stood at her side. Then, group by group, servants from the Kong Mansion, the Forest of Confucius, the Temple of Confucius, the stables and the lumberyard, and the Security Department would come in to kowtow and receive their gifts – a few hundred copper coins in a small red paper envelope. When one group had finished kowtowing and speedily withdrawn, the next group would enter. The endless kowtows and auspicious speeches were repeated ad infinitum until all the servants had paid their respects. Then, members of the family from the Twelve Mansions would start to arrive and the whole process begin again. After the family members came to the Mansion to pay their respects to us, we had to go and pay respects to them. From the year my elder sister married, when I was thirteen and my brother eleven, it fell to the two of us to pay respects outside the Mansion. Very often these obligations had not been fulfilled when our classes were due to begin, leaving us no choice but to continue the visits after class was over each day.

Starting on the first day of the lunar year and continuing for several days, the 'Drum Tower Gate Fair' was held each morning on the street running from the main gate of the Kong Mansion to the Drum Tower Gate. The fair was lively and bustling, with all kinds of things for sale as well as variety shows and performances by

[1]*Ruyi* are S-shaped, highly carved forms, about twelve inches long, sometimes translated as 'sceptres'. They are decorative and serve no purpose but they denote imperial favour as they were often bestowed as gifts by members of the imperial family. They symbolise the fulfilment of one's wishes because the two characters which form their name also mean 'as you wish'.

musicians, storytellers and martial-arts adepts. Each day we eagerly looked forward to watching the performances and never missed an opportunity to go.

The morning's Drum Tower Gate Fair gave way to the 'Dragon Lantern Gala' in the afternoon. Dragon lanterns, dry-land boat races, stilt-walking and lion dances were all very popular throughout the Qufu area. Dragon lanterns from the surrounding villages were brought into the Kong Mansion every year in festivities that lasted for many days. The fair was held in front of the Great Hall inside the Second Gate with townsfolk and villagers all squeezing in to watch the fun – it was one of the few chances we had each year to catch a glimpse of ordinary people. But to prevent us being crushed in the crowd we were not allowed to mingle with them and had to sit on a dais in the Great Hall.

During the Dragon Lantern Gala, footmen from the Kong Mansion and the 'fireworks family' would provide wonderful evening displays. There were also head masks that the Mansion servants put on and capered around in. There were two sets of the Eighteen Arhats,[1] as well as masks of dragons, tigers, cranes, the Laughing Buddha and little children.

Once when my elder sister was in her teens, she wanted to go out and join in the fun. We encouraged her to go, and she selected one of the lion's heads and put it on. The peasants were greatly amused and commented among themselves: 'The Kong Mansion's elder young lady is playing the lion.' The three of us were all delighted beyond words.

At the New Year we had one other opportunity to observe peasants: that was at the 'Forest Gate Fair' or 'Flower Market', held before the main gate of the Forest of Confucius outside the north gate of the town. On sale were Qufu's famous paper flowers, made by almost every family in the district, and sold as far away as Jinan and Beijing. Some were worn as decorations, some placed with

---

[1] Arhat is a Buddhist term meaning an enlightened being, a sort of Buddhist angel or saint who has achieved enlightenment through Buddhist practice. Traditionally there were 16 Arhats but the Chinese, in their sinified version of Indian Buddhism, added another two. They are often depicted in temples, each with his special attributes: one has extremely long eyebrows that he has to hold off the ground, another carries a three-legged fox or a mongoose, some are in meditative poses and all are very distinctively characterised.

offerings as part of a sacrifice and others made for arranging in flower-vases. My brother and sister and I went to the flower market once each year, but not to buy anything – the footmen already bought several boxes of flowers and put them in the Mansion – we simply made a circuit of the market in our sedan chairs and returned home. Watching from the sedan-chair windows, we were less interested in the flowers than in the people: we were generally cut off from the outside world and longed to know what other people were like. The clothing, manners and speech of peasants who were not descendants of a sage always became the topic of excited conversation once we arrived back home.

Apart from the New Year, my favourite festivals were the Mid-Autumn Festival (held on the fifteenth day of the eighth lunar month) and the Needlework-Begging Festival (held on the seventh day of the seventh month). On the evening of each of these festivals, tables were piled one on top of the other in the courtyard of the Qiantang Building with incense burners, sacrificial offerings and either moon cakes (at the Mid-Autumn Festival) or lucky fruits (sweet fried pastries made in various moulds) laid out on the uppermost table. People told us that because the offerings were placed so high they were closer to heaven, so Chang E,[1] the Jade Rabbit in the moon, and the Cowherd and Spinning Damsel[2] would be able to see them and would come down to eat. We believed every word of this, and each time the offerings were laid out, we stood near them in the courtyard watching the sky. Although we never saw anything, we continued to watch year by year, conjuring up pictures of how the beautiful immortals would drift down from their ethereal clouds to partake of our offerings.

After I married and left home, I lived in several busy, flourishing cities, but at New Year my thoughts would always turn to the

---

[1] Chang E was the wife of Hou Yi, the legendary archer, who had been given a bottle of the elixir of life by an immortal. When her husband was away hunting, she secretly drank the potion, and flew to the moon, where she lit the lamps every night. Her only companions were a Jade Rabbit which prepared her elixir and Wu Gang, sentenced to chop down a huge ever-growing cassia tree.

[2] The stars Altair and Vega, said to be a husband and wife called the Cowherd and Spinning Damsel. They were separated by the girl's angry parents after a secret liaison and permitted to meet once a year on the seventh day of the seventh month.

simple, rustic celebrations we held at home. Although the resplendent theatres in the big cities could boast of performers of great artistic skill, somehow they lacked the warmth of their humble counterparts in Qufu.

Mansion Cuisine

Mansion cuisine was as splendid as that produced in the imperial kitchens, but developed its own distinctive techniques. 'Mansion dishes' were widely renowned and found favour with the emperors who were regularly presented with Mansion delicacies to savour. Dishes at the Mansion were divided into many different grades and there were several different standards set for banquets. At the most lavish feasts, known as '*Gaobai* Banquets' or 'Full-scale Fêtes *à la* Kong Mansion', over 130 different dishes were served. Such lavish feasts were arranged for various emperors through the ages, as well as for such modern notables as Chiang Kai-shek, Kong Xiangxi (head of one of the 'Four Big Families') and Feng Yuxiang, the 'Christian General'.[1]

At these banquets, the guests sat on three sides of the table, while on the fourth side your *gaobai* were neatly arranged next to each other. *Gaobai* was a unique decoration used only at 'Full-scale Fêtes'. They were round, glutinous rice-flour pillars over a foot high and as wide as a rice bowl, each arranged on a silver dish. Arranged on the plate around the pillar was a kaleidoscopic pattern of tiny dried fruits and nuts (lotus seeds, shelled melon seeds, walnut kernels etc.) chosen for their contrasting colours and shapes. On the surface of each pillar, the inlaid fruits formed a single Chinese character. Read together, the characters on the four pillars made up the host's congratulatory message. If the feast celebrated a birthday, they might read 'Longevity Surpassing the South Mountain' or at a wedding 'Happiness, Longevity and Eternal Love'.

Arranging the dried fruits was a skill as delicate and painstaking

---

[1] The Christian General, so-called because of his apparent conversion to Protestantism (he used to mass-baptise his troops with a hose-pipe), was one of the northern warlords who through their military strength controlled much of China from 1911–1949; see note p. 126.

as fine embroidery. Four *gaobai* took twelve experienced chefs forty-eight hours to complete.

This kind of banquet had its own special cutlery and crockery of porcelain, silver or tin, all irreplaceable. Each time they were used, only servants considered particularly reliable were chosen to look after them. The shapes were all very unusual: there were square and cloud-shaped dishes, dishes shaped like ancient silver ingots . . . each selected according to the dishes served. There was one particular dish called 'taking the son to see the emperor' which was a duck and a pigeon side by side. 'Gold and silver fish' consisted of a white and yellow fish served on a plate shaped like two fish side by side, one yellow, one white. The small individual plates set before each guest were also variously shaped – like melons or the Eight Diagrams – according to their specific purpose.

One set of crockery included individual 'pools' for each guest. Each serving dish and rice bowl came in a dish of hot water that would keep the food warm for a long time. The bowls used for soup held only enough soup for a single mouthful. They were also placed in dishes of hot water.

Dishes for a 'Full-scale Fête' were cooked in accordance with a complete set of regulations. In ordinary feasts, the three most common dishes were 'the big three' – sea-cucumber, shark's fin and duck. Each of these was accompanied by four cold dishes, four hot dishes, four dishes to be eaten with rice, and then sweet dishes, cakes, pastries and fruit, about forty dishes in all.

The most humble feasts were held for the footmen and maidservants. Because they were not permitted to sit at a table, a large tent was erected in the Qianshang Building Courtyard in which the servants sat in a circle on the ground on freshly woven straw mats. According to the Mansion rules, each 'table' was given 'ten big bowls'. An old menu records these as: sea-cucumber, fish maw, stewed pork, shredded chicken, fish slices, boiled pork, meat pies, cabbage with shrimps, 'eight immortals' soup and sweet dishes.

Not all the dishes the Yansheng Duke ate were rare delicacies. One menu for the Duke lists six quite ordinary dishes along with *huhu* (salty maize gruel with vegetables), pancakes, sweet potato and salted vegetables – all commonly eaten by Shandong peasants, but made with better quality ingredients. My younger brother loved to drink *huhu*. When the Anti-Japanese War ended, he travelled

The Gate of the Inner Apartments, as seen from the inside

Ancient musical instruments in the Hall of Great Achievements

The kitchen of the Kong Mansion

The 'cloud and dragon' columns of the Hall of Great Achievements

The Forest of Confucius

back to Qufu from the south of China and as soon as he arrived home he asked for a dish of *huhu*.

Some very simple dishes were cooked for important guests because of their special significance. For example, beansprouts became a traditional Kong Mansion dish in the time of the Qianlong emperor. According to popular tradition, on one of the emperor's trips to Qufu he was offered a meal, but not being hungry, he scarcely ate anything. The Yansheng Duke became very anxious and ordered the chef to think of something. The cook was in a quandary: if His Majesty wasn't interested in their famous delicacies, what were they to do? He grabbed a handful of beansprouts and threw them in the pan with a few kernels of flower pepper (prickly ash). The emperor had never seen this spice before and asked the Yansheng Duke about it. The Duke told him it was a condiment used to bring out the flavour of foods. Qianlong tasted the beansprouts and praised them highly. The Duke took this as a great compliment and thereafter fried beansprouts became a traditional dish. But as time passed the simple dish underwent various developments until it became the 'lilac beancurd' served at banquets: the leaves were picked off each beansprout, leaving only the tender shoot. Beancurd was fried and cut into tiny triangles. After cooking, a piece of beancurd was placed with a beansprout in a way that made it resemble a lilac blossom. When the dish first arrived at the table, the host always placed the two together to demonstrate the likeness.

Among the families of hereditary servants at the Mansion was a 'beansprout trimmer family', whose special duty was to trim beansprouts for the Kong family. When I was young, however, the Kong Mansion was also supplied with beansprouts from the village.

After special processing, Kong Mansion herbs became a great delicacy at banquets and were frequently sent to court as gifts. We often ate them too, most common were shepherd's-purse and day-lily buds from the Rear Flower Garden, and a kind of wild sweet-potato from the Forest of Confucius.

The coarsest dishes at the Mansion were the pickles made in huge vats in the wintertime. Each year enough vegetables were processed to fill several rooms. I remember two rooms next to the Chuihua Gate in the Inner Apartments filled with large vats containing huge yellow 'drunken' crabs, pickled turnips and pickled cabbage. To prepare the latter, several layers of outer leaves were removed from the cabbage, leaving only the heart and surrounding tender leaves. Incisions were made in the base of the cabbage and spices forced into the centre. A heavy stone was placed on the vat to compress the pickles and a few weeks later the 'coral cabbage', so called because of its colour, was ready. Turnips were processed by making numerous deep incisions over the entire surface and then placing them in vats with sugar and vinegar. We ate little of these, since most of them were taken home by the servants.

I heard that apart from eating elaborate dishes, my father also loved to eat 'leftovers' – the remains of previous meals all mixed together – which he thought had a delicious sour flavour. There were two rich and influential families in Qufu, one named Sun and the other Jiang who had been local officials under the Qing dynasty, and with whom my father had frequent contact; whenever there was a wedding or birthday in one of these families, father would send a servant with a dish to collect some 'leftovers'. Of course they wouldn't think of really giving him leftovers, so they prepared a few special dishes and mixed them together, making sure they looked as much like leftovers as possible – otherwise father wouldn't enjoy them.

The Kong Mansion had three kitchens: the inner kitchen, the outer kitchen and the small kitchen. The inner kitchen provided food for the Inner Apartments; the outer kitchen cooked for the administerial assistants, managers, and accountants; and the small kitchen cooked solely for Madame Tao. In the summer, when we ate in the open-air pavilion in the Rear Flower Garden, a temporary kitchen would be set up there. The staff of the inner and outer kitchens were divided into three shifts, each working ten days a month. When I was a child, the heads of the three shifts that worked in the kitchens were Ge Wenhuan, Zhang Zhaozeng and Zhang Genguan. The three shifts would compete with each other to produce the best dishes so that they would be chosen to prepare banquets, for which there were rich rewards. At New Year or during sacrificial ceremonies, the three shifts would all be on duty simultaneously, working non-stop through the night. But they could spend their twenty-odd days off at home.

Work in the kitchen was finely divided among the kitchen staff. There were pastry cooks, cooks specialising in steaming meat-buns or pickling vegetables, beansprout growers . . . all specialist occupations handed down from generation to generation in a single family – sometimes for scores of generations. Chef Zhao Yuyan, now over seventy years of age, was still hale and hearty when I returned to Qufu in 1979. His ancestors had been cooks at the Mansion for a dozen or more generations. There was one chef called Wang Yuhuai who earned large monetary rewards as my father's favourite cook. He was highly skilled, and particularly adept at pastries and cakes. In variety, shape, taste and fragrance, Kong Mansion cakes and pastries far outstripped anything sold by Beijing's best-known shops at the time, and the family was fastidious about only eating cakes fresh from the oven. Kong Mansion pastries were often sent as gifts to the throne. Once Madame Tao was eating some of Wang Yuhuai's cakes when she noticed that they were of different sizes and called him in to explain. He said: 'I measured the dough with my hands, but the amounts are very accurate. Weigh them on a scale and if there's any difference between them, I'll take all the blame.' Madame Tao ordered a servant to weigh the cakes; sure enough, they were of identical weights.

The kitchens did not cook steamed bread. Each day a servant was sent to the Eastern College to collect it from the brewery which produced it and the rice wine used in sacrifices to Confucius. When weddings or funerals were held at the Mansion, large quantities of the bread were stored in the Inner Apartments.

When I was small, the Kong Mansion was already experiencing economic decline, so we couldn't ordinarily afford to eat those exquisite delicacies enjoyed by our ancestors. But each noon and evening when Madame Tao and we three children ate together, we still had seven or eight dishes. Several maidservants were on duty to carry dishes from the kitchen, bring them to the table, serve rice and take sundry orders. Although the inner kitchen was part of the Inner Apartments, to reach the Qiantang Building where we lived, the food had to be carried through several gates, along a long corridor and through several courtyards, so the dishes were always half cold by the time they arrived. In order to have our food hot in the wintertime, a chafing dish would be used. The four of us ate so little that a good half of the dishes were left over to be taken home by the maidservants. They arranged this according to a schedule and always knew whose turn it was next.

Legends

When I was three or four years old, the old people began to tell me stories about Confucius and our ancestors. I never read any children's stories, nor heard any tales other than these old legends steeped in mystery and superstition. My impression of Confucius was of a being something between man and deity, or a god who lived among mortals.

According to legend, before Confucius was born, his mother Yan Zheng went to Ni Mountain to pray for a son. His elder brother, Mengpi, had deformed feet making it impossible for him to officiate at sacrificial ceremonies so his mother wanted a second son. On her return home, a unicorn appeared in the courtyard and spat a silken scroll from its mouth which read: 'A star from heaven has come to earth to promote the vigour of the Zhou dynasty.' When Confucius was born, his parents named him Zhongni (Zhong, second son and Ni, the name of the mountain). Music floated down from heaven and five immortals descended sedately from the clouds. One of them proclaimed: 'Heaven gives birth to a sage; music descends from the skies.'

Confucius was said to be the Kui Star, the brightest star of the Big Dipper. According to the *Classic of Filial Piety*[1] this star determined the success or failure of literary works, and was regarded as the head of heavenly civil officials. Confucius was said to be this god of literature come down to earth and his library in the Temple of Confucius was thus called the Kui Literature Pavilion.

Since Confucius was a deity residing among mortals, he could naturally foretell the future. There was a popular story in Qufu about a prediction of his concerning Qin Shi Huang, the first emperor of China.[2] When Confucius was an old man, his son and

---

[1] *Classic of Filial Piety*: a work dating from the third or second century BC, included in the Thirteen Classics, an expanded version of the Five Classics and Four Books (see notes p. 63 and p. 8). Filial piety was one of the cornerstones of popular Confucianism and is described in the *Classic*: 'Filial piety is the root of all virtue . . . Our bodies, every hair and bit of skin are received by us from our parents . . . This is the beginning of filial piety. It commences with the service of parents; it proceeds to the service of the ruler.'

[2] Qin Shi Huang, who reigned as the first emperor of China (221–210 BC), had defeated all the other small states to unite China for the first time. Traditionally

disciples built a tomb for him, and on its completion invited him to inspect it. He was very satisfied, but his disciple Zi Lu said: 'The tomb is huge, like a mountain, and surrounded by many trees, but it needs a river to perfect it.' Confucius answered: 'There's no hurry, the Qin people will come and channel a river.'

Later when Qin Shi Huang ordered the burning of all books not concerned with law, medicine and science, and made a concerted attack on Confucianism, someone advised him: 'If you want to eliminate the influence of Confucius you must begin by destroying the *fengshui* of his tomb. There is no river in the Forest of Confucius; if you dig a stream between his tomb and his home, his sagely power will no longer be felt.' Qin Shi Huang took his advice and conscripted a body of corvée labourers to dig the Zhushui River, unwittingly rendering the sage a great service by completing the last item of construction for his tomb.

But in fact, Confucius himself was not superstitious. He said: 'Only at fifty does one understand the will of heaven', or the ways of the world. Obviously he had no powers of prophecy, but sought to learn the laws governing objective phenomena through careful study.

Seven of the buildings in the Kong Mansion are laid out in the shape of the Big Dipper, so one of the unique characteristics of Kong Mansion architecture is that it 'manifests the seven stars'. According to legend, there was a direct link between the Kong Mansion and the Big Dipper. Each year on the fourth day of the eighth month, the Yansheng Duke sacrificed to the constellation in a ceremony known as 'connecting with the Big Dipper'. The ceremony ensured that the link between heaven and the Kong Mansion remained unbroken, for only then could the Kong Mansion be said to be 'as long-lived as the heavens' as the couplet on the main gate proclaimed.

Compared with the resplendent majesty of the sacrificial ceremonies to Confucius, 'connecting with the Big Dipper' ceremonies were carried out in great secrecy. Not only were non-family

---

characterised as a ruthless despot who burnt all the existing books to eliminate criticism of his rule, he is now best known for his famous tomb outside Xi'an which comprises the buried terracotta 'army'.

members forbidden to participate, few of the inhabitants of the Kong Mansion knew anything about them.

On top of the wall outside the Qiantang Building was a small clock containing a mass of threads inside a glass case. On the fourth day of the eighth month, when the Big Dipper appeared in the sky, the Yansheng Duke and an aide who would carry the threads made contact with the constellation. The two men silently removed the threads from their case and went to the chapel to burn incense and offer sacrifices. The offerings were very simple: seven oil lamps arranged in the shape of the Big Dipper, five dishes of food and a handful of incense sticks. Once the offerings were laid out, the chapel attendant was dismissed leaving the two men alone. First the Yansheng Duke kowtowed, followed by his assistant, finally the threads were unrolled. There were yellow, white, black, green and red threads representing the five elements in accordance with ancient cosmological beliefs: Earth (yellow) produces Metal (White), Metal produces Water (black), Water produces Wood (green) and Wood produces Fire (red). The Duke's assistant tied the different coloured lengths together into a single, long thread, completing the connecting process. When Decheng carried out this sacrifice he was helped by Liu Mengying and only on his deathbed did Liu pass the secret of the ceremony on to his son Liu Sanyuan. Previously he had mentioned nothing about the ceremony to his son, for contacts between mortals and heaven cannot be discussed casually.

During the Tang dynasty, two famous fortune-tellers called Yuan Tiangang and Li Chunfeng were invited to the Kong Mansion to tell the fortunes of the coming generations of descendants. As the story goes, the two sat back to back, sketching sheet after sheet of symbols representing the fate of each generation. They then mixed all the sheets together and arranged them into one huge diagram called the 'back to back diagram'. I have seen this diagram: it was covered with a wide range of sketches – the sun, moon and stars; mountains and rivers; trees and plants; birds and beasts; household articles – all jumbled together in an incomprehensible manner. Amongst them was a small monkey carrying a peach. This, I was told, represented the seventy-seventh generation: my younger brother was born in the Year of the Monkey, after my father died, leaving only his mother Madame Tao (whose name is a homonym for peach – *tao*). At the time it occurred to me that there were so many pictures on the sheet that each generation was bound to find something appropriate on it. Yuan Tiangang and Li Chunfeng were extremely clever prognosticators.

Some of the stories are inspiring and unforgettable. Behind the Hall of Poetry and Rites in the Temple of Confucius, a broken wall over three metres high and fifteen metres long stands alone in the courtyard. This is the 'Lu Wall'. According to tradition, after unifying China at the close of the Warring States Period (476–221 BC), the first emperor of China, Qin Shi Huang, ordered 'the burning of the books and the suppression of Confucianism'. One day, the ninth generation descendant of Confucius, Kong Fu, received news from a trusted friend, Chen Yu, that the emperor was on his way to Shandong. Kong Fu owned many Confucian books inherited from his ancestors and being a descendant of the sage, his position was very tenuous. Following Chen Yu's advice, he began to make preparations. He and his disciples worked through the night concealing the Confucian classics in a hollow wall of the Ancestral Hall, and he then fled to live in seclusion as a teacher on Song Mountain. Later when two peasant conscripts, Chen Sheng and Wu Guang, rose in revolt against the Qin dynasty, Chen Sheng was delighted to receive him and lavished high honours upon him as a scholar and teacher. Kong Fu remained in the ranks of the army for two months until he died of illness in camp.

During the reign of the Han dynasty Jing emperor (147–141 BC), the Virtuous Prince of Lu decided to expand his palace and began to demolish the Kong Family Ancestral Hall. When his men reached this section of the wall they suddenly heard the sound of bamboo slats being rubbed against each other. They broke open the wall and found inside a huge store of books written on bamboo slats strung together with silken thread. The rest of the Ancestral Hall had already been demolished, but this wall was preserved for posterity. This is how the poetry and classics that were nearly destroyed by Qin Shi Huang were protected for succeeding generations.

The books in the Kong Mansion were believed to have had their own souls. There was an imperial library in the Eastern College, used to store all the poetry and classics presented to the Kong Mansion by emperors of various dynasties. When I was small, a spirit appeared in the building which was said to be some of the books transformed into a young woman. Everyone at the Kong Mansion called her 'the young wife from the imperial library'. She was beautiful and wore little wooden-soled shoes which several people had heard tapping on the floorboards of the building during the night. Some people had actually seen her too – just a brief glimpse before she disappeared from sight. It was said that she was invisible to anyone not familiar with the classics. I asked someone why the books changed into a young wife rather than an old man, and was quoted the famous saying: 'There are beautiful women in books,' an answer usually given to encourage boys to study hard for an official career that would bring wealth and a choice of beautiful wives. I loved watching the young wives in the operas staged at the Mansion and longed to see her, so I studied with renewed enthusiasm – but of course I never once caught a glimpse of her.

The Kong Mansion was also inhabited by a spirit in the form of an old man. Behind the Western College was an empty building called the Hall of the Tranquil Mind or the Nine Bay Room. From the outside it looked just like any other building, with carved and painted rafters and crossbeams, and partitions with doors and carved windows. But inside it was quite different. The ceiling and walls were hidden behind carved red-sandalwood grape trellises that divided the building into nine irregular bays. Before the building lay a secluded courtyard, tastefully laid out with flowers and plants. Under the ancient trees were yellow porcelain 'drum' stools and a small stone table. According to legend, on moonlit summer nights an old man with a long white beard came out of the Nine Bay Room where he lived and sat alone on one of the drums drinking wine. It was said that one of the old stewards had actually seen this old immortal drinking in the moonlight.

The Kong Mansion had hundreds of rooms that no one had entered for years – once a room was locked it might be a hundred years before it was reopened. Almost every room had its own 'spirits' and its legends of ghosts and supernatural beings. Rooms in which individuals had hanged themselves were haunted by ghosts for a long time afterwards. A huge snake that had coiled itself above the horizontal tablet over the door of one of the halls was believed to have practised Buddhism and become a deity. Even the unhaunted rooms in the wings had a mysterious air about them. When I walked through the long corridors past countless tightly-sealed rooms filled with books covered with thick layers of dust, I always felt that the books had turned into 'spirits'.

According to legend, all the spirits, ghosts, wraiths and goblins of the Kong Mansion were kept under control by the old immortal with the white beard. Since he preserved the peace at the Mansion, every year on New Year's Eve the Yansheng Duke would go alone to the Nine Bay Room to present him with sacrificial offerings. Accompanied by a servant carrying a lantern and plates of offerings, he would enter the hall, lay out the offerings, and then have the servant wait outside the door. Facing due north, he would then kowtow to show his respect. When my father performed this ritual in the Nine Bay Room, Liu Mengying acted as his assistant.

Although they were not haunted by ghosts, some of the buildings were enveloped in an air of mystery. The Tower of Refuge, which resembled a tall water tower, was built of solid black bricks and had no windows. Perhaps there was something special about the bricks, for they were said to be impervious to fire and cannon. The tower was built to provide the Yansheng Duke temporary shelter in times of turmoil. But it had never been used and the huge lock on the tiny door at the base of the building was encrusted with a thick layer of rust. People said that there was an ancient bottomless well inside the tower which had appeared at the command of heaven. Over the well was a wooden device to trap the unwary. One step on the wooden board and an unsuspecting intruder would be flipped into the well.

Few people ever ventured into the vicinity of the tower and its sole inhabitant was an owl whose strange cries floated through the air at night. Sometimes I would awake in the middle of the night and hear the watchman's gong and the far-off cry of the owl in the Tower of Refuge. I wondered whether the old man with the white beard had finished his wine and what was happening in the haunted rooms – maybe that snake was slowly slithering down from its perch . . . or maybe the young wife was clunking her way across the floor of the imperial library . . . Thoughts like these kept me awake for hours at night. When the oil lamps were lit every evening, a steward would call out loud: 'Shut the gates!' Only when the Chuihua Gate of the Inner Apartments was closed, and the ceremonial golden melons, axes and 'heaven facing stools' locked outside, did I get a feeling of peace and security.

Every evening at dusk, a great flock of crows would roost noisily in the branches of the ancient trees that filled the dark courtyards, and the next morning at first light they would all disappear. People said they were the 3,000 crow-soldiers that protected Confucius. Legend has it that when Confucius returned from his travels through several neighbouring kingdoms (*c.* 500 BC) he established a school in his home town and frequently took his disciples on pleasure trips outside the city. He loved to visit Ni Mountain and the Kunling Cave (Fuzi Cave, or Cave of the Master) where he was born. He would stand on the hillside above the cave gazing down on the Liao River as in the words of an old classic: 'The Master standing high above the river sighed: "It is thus that time passes." '

Since Confucius travelled frequently outside the city, he was often exposed to the danger of attacks by bandits and renegade soldiers. At such times, a huge flock of crows would swoop down from the sky and surround him to protect him. Confucius left the city early each day and didn't return until late at night. Likewise, the crows would fly out as soon as the city gates were opened and only return when they were about to be closed. Ordinary people had a superstition that crows were an evil omen, but they were always welcome at the Kong Mansion because of the legend that they had once protected Confucius. We often described the crows in the poetry we wrote as children.

We believed that birds had intelligence, and flowers minds of their own too. There was a species of yarrow plant with a straight stem and tiny white flowers growing in the Forest of Confucius that, together with the *Book of Changes*, was used in divination. Fortune-tellers who made use of these yarrow-stalks were considered especially perspicacious, thus soothsayers would go to any lengths to obtain yarrow-stalks from the Forest. It was said that if a fortune-teller hung a bunch of yarrow-stalks in front of his booth, this was an indication of his mastery of the art, and an easy means of boosting business. Visitors to the Forest of Confucius often took a few yarrow-stalks with them when they left and when I was small, I often picked them to tell my fortune.

Apart from yarrow, the Forest of Confucius was carpeted with *lingzhi* fungi,[1] which grew nowhere but inside the Forest.

---

[1] *Lingzhi fungus*, a fan-shaped growth, is thought to promote longevity and is highly prized as a medicine in China; because of its association with longevity, it is quite often depicted on porcelain with other lucky symbols like bats and deer.

When I went to the Forest as a child, I was struck by the fact that grass grew thickly on every grave mound except for that of Confucius. Maybe it was because the attendants at the Forest took special care of the sage's tomb, but the old people said that this phenomenon proved that Confucius' spirit remained alive after his death, another manifestation of his sagely powers.

There was also a special type of sweet-potato that grew wild in the Forest. It was in fact very similar to the cultivated sweet-potato, long and thin, rich in starch and very sweet. Ordinary folk were allowed to come and dig them out as a token of the 'benevolence' of the ancestors. We ate them ourselves and presented them to the court too.

Many objects in the Temple of Confucius were imbued with mystical power. I learned that a pearl once appeared in the mouth of a dragon on the pillar that stood before the portrait of Confucius in the Hall of Great Achievements. Each night it would glow so brilliantly that it illuminated the whole hall. This was the only 'glowing pearl' in China, and that it should have appeared not at the Imperial Palace but before the image of the sage was of great significance. During the Qing dynasty, the glowing pearl was stolen, and until I grew up, I thought of its loss with a great sense of regret.

Not only were the Kong Mansion and the Forest and Temple of Confucius shrouded in mystery, Qufu was also a magical place. In ancient times it was a vast stretch of forest called the Zhao Family Forest, but after the birth of Confucius it was said that the town sprung up, quite literally, overnight.

All the stories I heard as a child centred around my ancestors; and indeed I never heard any stories but these; when my daughter was small, the stories I told her all concerned my ancestors too, for those were the only stories I knew.

4

The First Family Under Heaven

The Clan

No accurate census of the entire Kong clan has ever been taken, but at present there are about 100,000 people surnamed Kong in the area around Qufu alone, not to mention those scattered by time and change throughout distant provinces. The largest branch of the family outside Qufu was established by Kong Yingda, nephew of the thirty-first generation direct descendant of Confucius, in Hebei Province and was known as the 'Clan West of the River'. Another branch was established when the forty-eighth generation eldest son Kong Duanyou followed the Song dynasty monarch south to Quzhou. Relatives of this Southern Clan now live in Sichuan, Jiangsu, Zhejiang, Jiangxi, Fujian and Anhui provinces. Kong Duanyou's younger brother remained at Qufu to safeguard the temple and his descendants carried on the line of Yansheng Dukes.

The Kong family at Qufu was usually known as the Queli Kongs and were divided into 'Inner' and 'Outer' Kongs. Direct descendants of Confucius himself were called Inner Kongs or Inner Courtyard Kongs while descendants of Kong Mo[1] were called Outer Kongs, Outer Courtyard Kongs or False Kongs (as they were originally not named Kong at all and only took on the name for appearance's sake), and excluded from the clan genealogy. This division, once distinct, has become obscured with time and many Kongs no longer know whether they are members of the inner or outer section of the family.

The Inner Kongs were further divided into sixty clan households

---

[1] Kong Mo, see pp. 107–8, not a true member of the family, murdered the forty-second generation Duke in AD 913. The murdered Duke's heir was reinstated and Kong Mo beheaded by imperial order in AD 930.

with the Yansheng Duke's family holding the highest position. The relationship between it and the other households was that of ruler and ruled, with the Yansheng Duke acting as the supreme leader of the entire clan. Particularly during the Ming and Qing dynasties, clan rules were extremely strict. A clan chief (a grade five official) appointed by the Yansheng Duke received a cane to symbolise his authority to rule the clan and worked in a special office in Qufu. I still remember the last clan head, Kong Chuanyu, an old gentleman with a white beard. By the time of the Republic,[1] there was very little work for him to do and he seldom came to the Mansion. Except when sacrificial ceremonies to Confucius were held we rarely thought about him. Only when the family register was being revised did he visit every day, hobbling slowly through the corridors and courtyards leaning on a walking stick. Later when the students of the Qufu Teachers' Training College staged the play *Confucius Meets Duchess Nanzi*, which casts derision on the life of Confucius, the old man became so furious that he fell ill and died.

The clan chief chaired a council of forty elders who were selected from amongst the close branches of the family for their noble character and high prestige to discuss and settle clan affairs. Each of the sixty households had two household heads who were responsible for sacrificial ceremonies and for settling intra-clan disputes. In the past the Qufu County Magistrate was appointed by the Yansheng Duke. During the reign of the Qianlong emperor, this practice ceased, but the County Magistrate still had to make his judgements in accordance with the Duke's instructions, which he would receive on a slip of paper. The County Magistrate had to implement clan rules, for offending the Yansheng Duke would mean the loss of his position.

Although the County Magistrate was ranked far below the Yansheng Duke, in the internecine struggles for power and advantage that were common among feudal government officials, he sometimes wielded more real power than his superior, and the Duke was powerless to control his actions. The seventy-first generation Yansheng Duke incurred disaster precisely for this reason.

In the Temple's Hall of Poetry and Rites hangs a tablet presented to the family by the Qianlong emperor in 1744. On it are inscribed

---

[1] i.e., after 1912.

thirty Chinese characters to be used as the first part of the given names of Kong family descendants. The whole clan was compelled to conform with this namelist and children named otherwise were omitted from the family register. Later my father added a further twenty characters to the list, had them approved by the Northern Warlord Government's Ministry of Internal Affairs and then had them proclaimed in every province and county throughout China.

The descendants of Mencius, Yan Hui and Zengzi (the latter two were favourite disciples of Confucius), all followed similar naming systems. They were also called 'sage's descendants' and their eldest sons were hereditary Doctors of the Five Classics at the Imperial Academy. Their relationship with the Kong family was like that between the low ranking and high ranking households of a single clan. Their memorials to the throne were first submitted to the Yansheng Duke who passed them on to the throne. Whenever the Yansheng Duke went to the capital to visit the emperor, he always took these sage's descendants with him. Although never granted an audience by the emperor, they accompanied the Yansheng Duke in performing the rites at the Imperial College and performing duties at the Ying Terrace.

Clan rules were laid down by the Kong Mansion as follows: 1. Sacrifices to the ancestors must be abundant, clean, sincere and conducted respectfully. 2. Fathers must show kindness, sons be filial, elder brothers be fraternal and younger brothers be respectful. 3. Revere Confucianism and value the Way, delight in performing the rites and esteem moral virtue. 4. Be prompt about making rent payments. 5. Men of the Kong clan shall not be slaves, the women shall not be servants. 6. Read literature and know the classics, bring glory to your parents, do not sink into vulgarity and content yourself with a humble position.

Because of the fifth rule, all clan members who worked as servants had to change their names and could not be listed on the family register. There were several former clan members working as servants at the Mansion, all of whom changed their names upon commencing their duties.

Restrictions on the women of the clan were particularly severe. They were not permitted to marry a second time or to take part in sacrificial ceremonies. The rules governing marriage stipulated that a woman must remain faithful to a dead husband throughout her life, a restriction which led to tragedy for many women. One of the descendants of Yan Hui was betrothed to Kong Wenxun, but before the marriage took place, Kong died and the seventeen-year-old girl, out of loyalty, hanged herself. A memorial archway was built outside the gate of the Forest of Confucius to commemorate her chastity. There were many such memorial archways around Qufu. Another story tells of a 'Mistress Chaste and Virtuous' of the Fourth Kong Mansion. When her betrothed suddenly died, she married his memorial tablet. After the ceremony, she retired to the nuptial chamber where she changed her bridal clothes for mourning gowns and remained a widow until her death, never once leaving the courtyard where she lived. A third story tells how when the army of the Eight Allied Forces invaded northern China in 1900 one of the Kongs of the Fifth Mansion led troops into battle and rather than admit defeat, chose to cut his own throat. When the news reached home, his son hanged himself as an act of filial piety and after the body was prepared for burial, his wife hanged herself as a symbol of her chastity and devotion. The emperor presented a wooden tablet to the household reading: 'A family replete with loyalty and filial piety.' When I was a child, the tablet still hung over the door. Tragedies like these were common during the Ming and Qing dynasties.

The Kong Clan Register is the oldest and most complete family register in China. Since the middle of the Song dynasty (around 1080) when the register was begun, it has been regularly revised every thirty years, with a major revision taking place every sixty years. My grandfather made minor revisions to it, and the last revision was made by my brother Kong Decheng.

This final revision was unusual in that it was over 100 years late. The last major revision had been carried out by Kong Jifen of the Twelfth Mansion in 1744, but he was falsely accused of writing seditious literature and banished to serve in the army in Xinjiang where he later died. From that time on the register had not been thoroughly revised again.

When my brother was seven years old, my stepmother, Madame Tao, and the council of elders decided to bring the register up to date, and after two years of preparatory work set up the 'National Office for the Revision of the Kong Clan Register'. As supreme head of the clan, Kong Decheng was the nominal director-general of the operation, but it was in fact run by the clan chief Kong Chuanyu and two of the members of the council of elders, Kong Yinqiu and Kong Jilun. The office was officially opened in the autumn of 1930 and representatives from branches of the Kong clan poured into Qufu from all over the country. The usually cold and cheerless Kong Mansion suddenly overflowed with bustle and noise. The solemn opening ceremony was held in the Hall of Poetry and Rites in the Temple of Confucius. With the seven-year-old Kong Decheng clad in ancient ceremonial robes at their head, the elders and clan members involved in the revision work knelt facing north to report their intentions to the spirits. Kong Chuanyu read out the oath to revise the family register and then placed the document among the incense burners on the long altar. The worshippers then performed the three genuflections and nine kowtows and finally, in strict order of seniority paid their respects to Decheng. Afterwards a feast was held in the Great Hall. A coloured marquee had been set up in front of the hall where musicians played and firecrackers were let off. Although it was out of bounds for women, I skipped in and out as happy and excited as if it were the New Year.

After seven years of work the revised register was completed in 1937. At the closing ceremony in the Hall of Poetry and Rites in the Temple of Confucius, the register was placed on the altar and Decheng led the clan to the Requite Ancestral Kindness Hall to inform the spirits. After paying their respects in the Hall of Poetry and Rites, the officials in charge presented the register to Decheng who received it on his knees. Behind him the clan members knelt respectfully in order of seniority. Then in the same order they paid their respects to Decheng. This was followed by great feasting and celebrations, and Decheng was photographed with all the clan representatives to commemorate the occasion.

The Twelve Mansions

When the eldest son of the Yansheng Duke by his legal wife inherited his father's title and set up his home in the Kong Mansion, his brothers, according to a Qing practice, all had to leave their old home and live in one of the 'Twelve Outer Mansions'.

The Outer Mansions in fact totalled only nine in number. The number of each Mansion referred to the seniority of the brother who had lived there first. Thus there were the Great Mansion, where the eldest son by the Yansheng Duke's concubine had lived, as well as the second, third, fourth, fifth, seventh, eighth, tenth and twelfth mansions, where other brothers had lived. The Yiguan Hall inside the Kong Mansion was also counted as a separate household because there was not enough room outside the Mansion to accommodate the whole family.

Besides receiving a house, the brothers were also presented with a small plot of land. They had no official title, though under the Ming dynasty, the second son was made a hereditary Doctor of the Five Classics at the Imperial Academy and the third son was made a hereditary Doctor of the Board of Supreme Ritual. Because they had neither a hereditary official stipend nor much land to support them they led a very unstable economic existence.

My father and grandfather were both only sons, so the Twelve Mansions were all occupied by quite distant relatives – among the closest relations was my father's cousin Kong Lingyu who lived in the Fifth Mansion. When my father died, he requested in his last memorial to the President of the Republic and ex-emperor that Kong Lingyu should handle the affairs of the Mansion in his place, and accordingly he and his wife and daughter moved in with us. His wife, Madame Yuan, was the younger sister of Yuan Shikai, an amiable woman who minded her own affairs and got on very well with my brother and me. She had no sons, so when she died Decheng 'smashed the plate' at her funeral in place of the eldest son.

The rules governing relations between the Twelve Mansions and the Duke's Mansion were very strict and relatives could not casually visit one another as friends and neighbours do today. Personal relationships were all institutionalised. Because Confucius' thought centred around the rites, the Kong clan emphasised etiquette in all areas of life and a man's moral worth was measured by the degree of his conformity to these set rules. In the early Qing dynasty, the family published a complete and extremely strict set of family rituals entitled *The Kong Clan Rites*, but it was banned by the Qianlong emperor and as a result the rituals themselves became less rigid. When I was small the old protocol was still observed and relatives had to wait for official notification of festivals, weddings or funerals before they could come to the Duke's Mansion to offer congratulations or condolences. There were rules governing the giving and receiving of gifts between households that were passed down unchanged through the ages. For example, when a child was born, gifts had to be made of rice, eggs, brown sugar, noodles, glutinous rice candies and cakes. Gold and silver foil was to be sent on the death of a family member. Relatives from the Twelve Mansions visiting the Kong Mansion had to be offered eleven plates of light refreshments and be entertained with a feast including the 'three great dishes' – sea-cucumber, shark's fin and duck – as well as four accompanying cold dishes, four hot dishes and finally four dishes to be eaten with rice.

Guests were received in different places according to their status: close relatives were received in the East Building while distant relatives were received in the West Building; male guests were received in the Flowery Hall while women were received in the Inner Apartments. The formalities on meeting were extremely elaborate. Younger generations, attended by servants standing ready with yellow satin cushions, knelt on the ground and bowed in respect to their elders.

When the Kong Mansion had news to communicate, a gong was sounded thirteen times in the street, while the Twelve Mansions were permitted seven strokes of the gong. If a member of one of the families had committed a crime, the family was not permitted music at funerals or weddings. Because a member of the Eighth Mansion had committed a crime, his family were only permitted to beat drums at important celebrations. After the founding of the Republic in 1912, this custom gradually died out.

The Marriage of a Princess

Brothers of the Yansheng Duke were not allowed to live at the Kong Mansion, but nevertheless there was a family of distant relatives who lived generation after generation in a large section of the Mansion's Eastern College. This was the Yu family of 'official relatives' who had moved into the Mansion during the reign of the Qianlong emperor (reigned 1736–1796).

Eleven emperors of six Chinese dynasties visited the Kong Mansion, but among them the Qianlong emperor stands out for having made the journey nine times. Qianlong had a daughter by the Filial, Holy and Virtuous Empress, whom he loved very dearly. This princess had a dark mole on her face which fortune-tellers predicted would bring great misfortune unless she married into a family more illustrious than either the nobility or the highest of officials. The emperor had no other choice but to marry her into the Kong house, for only the Yansheng Duke could walk beside the emperor along the Imperial Way in the Palace and only at the Kong Mansion did the emperor perform the three genuflections and nine kowtows to ancestors other than his own. Thus on his first visit to the Mansion, Qianlong made arrangements for the marriage. But Manchus and Chinese were not permitted to intermarry, so the emperor was obliged to first give his daughter into adoption by the family of the mandarin Yu Minzhong, whereupon she married the seventy-second generation Yansheng Duke, Kong Xianpei, in 1772. The Kong clan all addressed her as Madame Yu.

For three months before the wedding, items of the princess' dowry arrived daily at the Kong Mansion. Besides several thousand trunks of clothing and jewellery alone, there were innumerable boxes of ginseng, coral, ivory carvings, jade miniature landscapes, etc. Large-scale construction was begun at the Mansion. The eight-acre Tieshan Garden was built at the back of the Inner Apartments, and exotic plants and trees were brought from all over the country for its specially built hot-house. Accompanying the princess to her new home were several court eunuchs whose wages were provided for by tax revenue collected in some twenty villages that formed part of her dowry. The family of the princess' foster father Yu Minzhong also moved into the Kong Mansion and from that time on, lived there generation after generation.

As the wedding day drew near, Kong Xianpei went personally to the capital to receive his bride. At an audience with the Qianlong emperor he was presented with gifts of pelts, twenty-seven metres of satin, five scrolls of fine writing-paper, an inkslab, four boxes of brushes and two containers of red seal ink. The empress also summoned her new son-in-law to audience and presented him with a jasper *ruyi* (symbolising the fulfilment of all one's wishes), four marten pelts, an official's necklace of precious stones, three pairs of embroidered purses and a set of glass bottles and bowls. As the princess was about to leave, the empress summoned her and presented her with an imperial jasper *ruyi* and a satin purse embroidered with the character 'longevity', handkerchiefs, cosmetics and adornments.

On the occasion of the marriage, imperial officials came forward to offer congratulations and precious gifts. Among the officials was the magistrate of a prefecture who sent only a small gold axe. On being asked by the emperor the significance of his gift, he replied that it was to be used by the future imperial grandchildren to crack walnuts. Qianlong was delighted with this answer and declared the axe the best of the presents received. Gold and silver counted for little at the Kong Mansion, but by virtue of the emperor's pronouncement, the little gold axe became a treasured family heirloom.

After the wedding, the emperor, empress and empress dowager visited the Kong Mansion and were met at Dezhou by a party led by Kong Xianpei and his father, Kong Zhaohuan, including the descendants of Yan Hui, Mencius and Zengzi, and the princess, her mother-in-law Madame Cheng, and Kong Zhaohuan's mother, Madame He. Whilst at Qufu, the emperor lodged in a study at the Temple of Confucius and also took his meals at the Temple. Although the study was not particularly well-appointed, it was the sacred place where the Yansheng Duke bathed and rehearsed the rites before offering sacrifices to Confucius, and thus it was deemed fit to serve as temporary quarters for the emperor.

Each time the emperor came he would both present and receive gifts. Whatever he brought, valuable or trifling, was first enshrined on an altar and recorded in the Kong Mansion archives. At different times, the emperor presented a plate of apples, a jar of osmanthus-flower cookies and on nineteen different occasions sent special Manchurian digestive foods and toffee-covered crab-apples.

The princess did not get on well with her mother-in-law. She considered herself far above Madame Cheng, especially as she was not Kong Xianpei's natural mother, but only his step-mother. In addition Kong Xianpei's paternal grandmother and great-grandmother were both still alive, which relegated Madame Cheng to the third position among the women of the household. The princess showed her little respect and Madame Cheng was not prepared to make concessions to improve their relations, so the situation deteriorated until Madame Cheng made bold to complain about her lack of filial submission directly to the Qianlong emperor. Little had she guessed that the doting father, already distressed by his favourite daughter's marriage into a faraway Shandong family, instead of disciplining the princess merely remarked: 'Her temper has always been the same. There's no need to tell me. I know.' After this the women are said to have become even more incompatible.

At each of the princess' birthdays, the Qianlong emperor would send officials to wish her a long life and present gifts, and on the death of the empress, Kong Xianpei and his wife and father went personally to the capital with a burial gift of a coffin of catalpa wood. The Qianlong emperor subsequently made several more visits to Qufu and the close ties between the court and Kong Mansion were sufficient to reveal the fact that the princess in fact held a position higher than any other person in the Mansion.

The princess bore no children, but adopted a nephew to be the next Yansheng Duke. The birth of this child, Kong Qingrong, was very long and difficult, prompting the princess to deduce that the baby must have in spirit been intended for her. Thereupon she ordered all the gates of the Mansion to be opened and a bow and arrow to be hung over the Main Gate. The south gates of Qufu which stood directly opposite the Temple of Confucius were also opened. When the newly born child was brought to the princess' rooms, a message was sent to the emperor announcing the birth of a grandson. This was my great-grandfather Kong Qingrong.

Kong Qingrong was always very respectful and attentive to the princess and served her constantly when she fell ill. After her death the Daoguang emperor (reigned 1821–1851) sent officials to make sacrifices and erected a wooden memorial archway in her memory inscribed 'The call of the phoenix acclaims virtue'.[1] Tablets commemorating the family ancestors were usually placed in the Requite Ancestral Kindness Hall (the family temple), and on the first and fifteenth day of each new year and the anniversaries of the births and deaths of close relatives, we would go and kowtow to them in veneration. The princess' tablet however, was not placed there but in a specially built temple in the Eastern College called the Hall for Cherishing Ancestral Kindness. Each day three meals were punctually placed before the tablet, and numerous servant girls washed

---

[1] The phoenix was the symbol of empresses; the dragon of emperors.

and attended it as if it were a living person. I never saw this strange ritual for during my childhood the temple was only frequented by its watchmen. This was probably one of the changes brought about by the founding of the Republic.

My great-grandfather was a well-known scholar who left to posterity a wealth of poetry, prose and paintings, the best of which are *Poems from Tieshan Garden* and *Sketches from Tieshan Garden*. Tieshan (Iron Mountain) Garden, also known as the Rear Flower Garden, was so named by Kong Qingrong because slabs of iron-ore[1] were brought to the garden for its reconstruction during the reign of the Jiaqing emperor (1796–1821). Kong Qingrong also gave himself the style 'The Master of Tieshan Garden'.

Although these slabs were new to the Mansion, myths soon began to grow up around their origins. According to one story they had grown out of the ground like shoots of bamboo and had changed into iron-ore because there was treasure in the ground below. I was very familiar with this story as a child and believed it implicitly. Every time I went to the garden I would always look carefully around the stone slabs to see if any other rare treasures had sprung out of the earth. The impression this left on me is very strong and every mention of Kong Qingrong reminds me of the iron mountains and those innocent fantasies of my childhood.

But returning to Kong Qingrong, I must admit I have never seen copies of either *Poems from Tieshan Garden* or *Sketches from Tieshan Garden*, though I have read numerous scattered lines of his poetry which probably originate from these two books. The Mansion also contains several inscribed horizontal tablets and paired couplets written by him. He is said to have been friendly with men of renown from all over the country and often invited them to the Kong Mansion to compose poetry and paint.[2] They always

---

[1]Rocks (for use as decorative rocks/rockery) hollowed out by water, stalactites and other weird natural formations were highly prized in Chinese gardens, either set together in rockeries or mounted on pedestals.

[2]Such gatherings where scholars drank, wrote or admired poetry or paintings, have a long history in China. The great Tang poet Li Bai (or Li Po, AD 701–762) was extremely fond of wine and often included it in his verse and these aristocratic literary gatherings are frequently celebrated in the literati painting of the Ming (AD 1368–1644) and Qing (AD 1644–1911).

gathered in the Western Flowery Hall where Kong Qingrong had hung couplets of his own composition before the door: 'The thirst for wine, the passion for poetry, restrain them not, for today we enjoy today's sunshine,' and, 'Flowers at dawn and the moon at dusk; this scene is like the spring of years gone by.' He could drink great quantities of wine and was nicknamed 'the third drinker' by his scholar friends. He even chose a scholarly wife for his only son Kong Fanhao – the famous Qing dynasty realist painter Bi Jingheng.

The princess' relatives, the Yu family, lived continuously at the Kong Mansion, but had little interaction with the Kong clan. When I was young they had already been reduced to destitution, surviving on a monthly ration of grain donated from the Kong Mansion granaries. I occasionally went to their house to play, but it was a desolate place inhabited only by one woman and her daughter-in-law. The menfolk were away finding whatever work they could, and rarely had the chance to come home.

A Family Martyr

Outside the Main Gate of the Forest of Confucius, a lonely grave lies hidden among the wild grass at the edge of the road. This is the grave of Kong Jisu, the great Qing dynasty calligrapher. His work *Calligraphy Models from Jade Rainbow House* is a national historical treasure which received wide acclaim from both domestic and foreign aficionados when it was exhibited in Beijing in 1979.

Kong Jisu[1] was a man of exceptional talent who devoted his life to scholarly research, but met with nothing but misfortune. A close relative of the Yansheng Duke, he lived at the Twelfth Mansion, but because he was accused of betraying the court and the Yansheng Duke and plotting to seize power, he was expelled from the clan and condemned as a criminal by both the court and clan. After his death he was not permitted to be buried in the Forest of Confucius and his coffin was bound and locked with three iron chains to symbolise his guilt.

When I was a child, the clan elders used to talk about the 'crimes' of Kong Jisu, none of which in fact stemmed from his own

---

[1] A seventieth generation descendant who lived in the mid-eighteenth century.

words or actions – they were all founded on absurd feudal superstition.

As the story goes, one night someone in the Beijing Imperial Palace suddenly discovered that the Ziwei Star, which represented the fate of the emperor, was gradually fading and being replaced by an exceptionally bright star in close proximity. After careful calculations, the diviners determined that the star represented someone in Shandong and further sorcery specified him as Kong Jisu. The emperor immediately sent officials to Qufu to search for the man and make an investigation. As a result they discovered that the Twelfth Mansion where Kong Jisu lived was constructed on the model of the Eight Diagrams used in divination, and that the roof ridges of the nine principal rooms were connected, all of which were considered taboo. As punishment they not only smashed the roof ridges, but dug up the graves of Kong Jisu's parents. Buried in the ground to the left and right of the tombs they claimed to have discovered large creatures like dragons, each missing a talon. According to the diviners, when the talons grew to full size, Kong Jisu would be able to seize power and usurp the throne. At this time the Kong family also discovered that the main branches of the cypress tree outside the Hall of Great Achievements in the Temple of Confucius were withering while the smaller branches were luxuriant. It was explained that this was because Kong Jisu was reciting incantations to destroy the Yansheng Duke so that he as the second brother could seize the dukedom. The withering of the tree's main branches symbolised that the Yansheng dukedom would not be inherited by the former duke's eldest son, but by his second son. The clan declared Kong Jisu guilty of 'reciting incantations to start a second branch' and Kong Jisu, now a confirmed 'criminal', was expelled from the clan.

For ten years after his expulsion from the clan, Kong Jisu remained inside the Jade Rainbow House where he devoted himself to researching calligraphy and compiling and engraving the famous 500 *Calligraphy Models from Jade Rainbow House*. As an old man he travelled to Beijing where he died of illness. Because he had never been absolved of his crimes, his coffin was bound by three iron chains and transported back to Qufu where it was buried in waste ground outside the Forest of Confucius. Not even his descendants were able to escape the reputation of being a 'criminal family' and were punished by being forbidden to play any instruments but a drum at weddings and funerals. The prohibition was observed for eight generations until my father inherited the Yansheng dukedom under the Republic. The family was to hold a funeral and someone asked my father whether or not they should only beat drums. Father replied: 'We live in a republic now, if you think you ought to play instruments then play them!' – only then did they resume playing instruments.

Although the Kong Clan expelled Kong Jisu, they still regarded his calligraphy as one of the treasures of the Kong Mansion and the *Calligraphy Models from Jade Rainbow House* was moved to the Fifth Mansion for safe keeping. When my elder sister and I were married, rubbings of the *Calligraphy Models from Jade Rainbow House* were sent to Beijing as part of the dowry quite unique to the Kong Mansion.

The fate of Kong Jisu's brother Kong Jifen was even more tragic. Kong Jifen spent his life researching the history of the Kong Clan and wrote many scholarly works; at the age of twenty-one, he compiled a twenty-two *juan*[1] *Genealogy of the Family of Confucius Compiled in 1744 During the Reign of the Qianlong Emperor.* Later he also compiled *A Study of Queli Literature* in 100 *juan*; *A Complete Record of Music and Dance; Funeral Rites; Notes on Queli Ceremonies; A Short Genealogy of the Direct Descendants of Confucius; Random Poetry*, etc.

At the age of fourteen, he first became a student and later served as a secretary at the Imperial College and an official at the Privy Council. When the Qianlong emperor came to Qufu, Kong Jifen discussed the classics with him in the temple of Confucius, acted as his guide and in general made a very favourable impression. Whenever there were marriages or funerals in the clan, he would be asked to explicate the rites. To ensure that there would be set rules for each ceremony, he collected detailed materials and after three years of work finished the fourteen-volume *Kong Clan Ceremonial Rites* and the four-volume *Answers to Questions on Family Rites*, never imagining that they would bring about his downfall and death.

A grade five official in the clan named Kong Jishu submitted a

---

[1] A *juan* or booklet-like division of a larger work similar to our 'chapter' or 'section'.

report to his superiors denouncing the rites described in *Kong Clan Ceremonial Rites* as differing from the Qing court rites as laid down in the official manual, *Complete Book of Ceremonies*, and accusing Kong Jifen of having the effrontery to tamper with the ceremonial rites fixed by the court. He interpreted a phrase in the author's preface, 'from a sincere desire to return to the ways of the ancients', as being an expression of dissatisfaction with contemporary society and a proposal to restore the rule of the Ming dynasty. Under the Qianlong emperor, subversive literature was dealt with in a swift and severe fashion, so on receiving the letter of accusation, the Governor of Shandong immediately sent a report on the matter to the throne and rushed to Qufu where he had Kong Jifen arrested and taken to the provincial capital for interrogation. Later, on the orders of the emperor, Kong Jifen was taken under escort to Beijing and handed over to the Ministry of Punishments where he was again interrogated rigorously by the Prime Minister and other top officials. Kong Jifen repeatedly protested that *Kong Clan Ceremonial Rites* referred only to family ceremonies and that 'restoring the ways of the ancients' simply advocated returning to the ways of Confucius. Since the Qing court also revered Confucius as a sage, the statement implied nothing about past and present social systems. But these explanations failed to reduce his guilt in the eyes of his judges and in accordance with a suggestion from the Qianlong emperor, they passed the following sentence:

> Kong Jifen, a descendant of the sage, once listed on the register of officials, whose family have for generations received imperial favours, has written the unauthorised *Kong Clan Ceremonial Rites* in order to win a name for himself. Just as His Majesty has stated: 'A scoundrel like this who has no respect for propriety is the most despicable of beings.' Furthermore, all ceremonial rites have already been formally stipulated in *Complete Book of Ceremonies* and ceremonies must follow this clear pattern . . . Kong Jifen should be punished with the utmost severity and is sentenced to hard labour in the Ili Valley as a warning to others who knowingly write unauthorised works. Aside from the wooden printing blocks of *Kong Clan Ceremonial Rites*, which have already been destroyed by the Governor of Shandong, all copies of the book must be sought out and destroyed.

Kong Jifen, already over sixty, was put in a cangue, handcuffed and sent to labour with the army in the Ili Valley in distant Xinjiang. Sixteen months after being sentenced, he died, probably still on his way to join the army.

After the sentence was passed on Kong Jifen, *Kong Clan Ceremonial Rites* was classified as a banned book, and on Qianlong's orders, the Governor of Shandong came to Qufu and for several months carried out a large-scale investigation and confiscation. The Yansheng Duke, Kong Xianpei, issued a notice to the whole clan ordering:

> All members of close and distant branches of the clan who have in their possession copies of *Kong Clan Ceremonial Rites* or any other books written by Jifen must immediately surrender them to the authorities. Anyone discovered to be concealing copies of these books, or showing reluctance to submit them, will be punished severely.

Several members of the clan were interrogated and had their homes closely searched. The heads and office holders of the sixty Kong clan families each had to write a statement guaranteeing that their families had complied with the Duke's orders.

Amongst the tens of thousands of volumes that constitute the Kong family archives, there is almost no reference to Kong Jifen, probably a deliberate attempt to cover up the family scandal. I only learned a little about him through casual conversations with older members of the clan.

Whenever I think of Kong Jifen and Kong Jisu, my heart fills with sorrow and indignation. Living in a hereditary aristocratic family in an environment of privilege and ease, they did not allow themselves to sink into self-indulgence, preferring instead to dedicate their lives to scholarship, and in this gained notable success – a rare achievement in those times. But while alive they both suffered persecution, and even after death were denied the high acclaim they deserved. The key to their fate lay with their chief adversary, the daughter of the Qianlong emperor (reigned AD 1736–1796), whom they had been honoured to receive as a bride at the Kong Mansion.

According to several of the family elders, the two brothers' misfortunes did not come upon them by chance, but were the result of sharp contradictions between members of the clan.

Kong Jihu, the eldest son of the sixty-eighth generation Yansheng Duke, Kong Chuanfeng, died while still in his twenties and shortly afterwards, Kong Chuanfeng became seriously ill and passed the dukedom on to Kong Jihu's eldest son, Kong Guangqi. Kong Chuanfeng and his second wife Madame Xu then moved into the Twelfth Mansion with their two younger sons Kong Jifen and Kong Jisu. On his succession, the young Yansheng Duke was only twelve years old and made daily visits to the Twelfth Mansion to pay his respects and ask for personal advice. Kong Chuanfeng was old and frequently ill, so the routine affairs of the Mansion were taken care of by the Duke's two uncles, Kong Jifen and Kong Jisu. At the time there were said to be treasures in the Twelfth Mansion unequalled by those of the Kong Mansion and by all accounts real power in the Kong Clan and the Kong Mansion lay in the Twelfth Mansion. When Kong Guangqi died, his son Kong Zhaohuan carried on what was now a family tradition of daily visits to pay respects and discuss affairs with his two grand-uncles. The custom had been observed for several decades before Kong Zhaohuan's son, Kong Xianpei, married the Qianlong emperor's daughter, but on her arrival at the Kong Mansion she assumed a social position above the entire clan and could not bear to see the real power of the Mansion fall into the hands of others. Had the daily visits to the Twelfth Mansion been a mere formality for the Yansheng Duke, this alone would have represented enough of a lowering of his status to arouse the princess' ire, let alone the situation where Kong Jifen and Kong Jisu had gradually taken over the running of the Mansion. Naturally, the princess was eager for a chance to discredit the two men in her father's eyes, so it is not surprising that Qianlong should say that although Kong Jifen 'had ability', he was 'too fond of minding other people's business'. Thus when the Ministry of Punishments submitted the memorial recommending that Kong Jifen should join the army, the emperor gave it his approval on the same day. But quite clearly the reasons for Qianlong selecting Kong Jifen's case out of numerous similar cases for particularly severe punishment were two-fold.

Kong Jifen's son, Kong Guangsen, was a famous Qing dynasty philologist, whose works have been preserved to the present day in the Beijing Library, but because of his unfortunate uncle, he was unable to enjoy the fruits of a successful career. Several times he risked his life in concealing copies of *Kong Clan Ceremonial Rites* during searches of the Mansion, but unfortunately these were later destroyed during the turbulence of China's recent 'cultural revolution'.

Kong Clan Ceremonial Rites and *Answers to Questions on Family Rites* were each divided into four sections. Part One dealt with rituals at the Apricot Altar, sacrifices at the Temple, details about coffins and memorial ceremonies at tombs. Part Two discussed funeral rites, mourning apparel, funeral sacrifices, the importance of returning home to carry the coffin of a parent or grandparent, the re-interring of bodies, the funeral procession itself, and included a table describing the specific type of mourning attire to be worn by various relatives of the deceased. Part Three was concerned with commendatory rites, marriages, family feasts, and procedures for revising the family register. The fourth part was a postscript written by the author.

Kong Clan Ceremonial Rites and *Answers to Questions on Family Rites* were written for the purpose of perpetuating feudal clan rites, but if they had been preserved to this day they would have provided us with valuable reference material for research on Confucius and feudal society.

Although the Kong Mansion and Kong clan stressed etiquette and had elaborate rituals for every kind of social occasion, after Kong Jifen's books were banned they had no standard reference work to consult. In the reign of the Xuantong emperor (1908–1911) and under the rule of Yuan Shikai, a *Manual of Martial Dances, Ceremonies for Worshipping the Sage* and descriptions of official uniforms to be worn in ceremonies in honour of Confucius were issued, and in the early years of the Republic, Professor Ma Jiming of Beijing University, who studied the Kong Mansion funeral ceremonies, wrote *Regulations for Burials in the Forest of Confucius*. But these are the only extant works on the subject.

Because Qufu had been a centre of classical culture since the Spring and Autumn Period (770–476 BC), and because Chinese emperors throughout the ages had always revered Confucius, there were naturally a large number of scholars in the Kong clan; but like Kong Jisu, Kong Jifen and Kong Guangsen, most were frustrated in their attempts at scholastic careers. Kong Shangren was another such scholar. He was the grandson of a *linsheng* (a salaried student of a county-level school) renowned for having spent sixty years studying without once leaving his house. His father was a Ming dynasty Second Degree (provincial level) graduate who retired from his post and lived in seclusion in protest against official corruption. Kong Shangren grew up with his father and grandfather and although he sought scholarly honour, failed the examinations several times. In disappointment, he retired to the seclusion of Shimen (Stone Gate) Mountain.

Five years later, when the Kangxi emperor (reigned 1662–1722) came to Qufu, the Yansheng Duke, Kong Yuqi, asked Kong Shangren to lecture the emperor on the classics and act as his guide. Kangxi was impressed by the scholar and appointed him to a post in the Imperial College. Leaving his home, Kong Shangren took up office in Beijing where he learned much about society and evoked the displeasure of the throne by writing several poems reflecting the sufferings of the working people. In the poem *Beggar at the Post House* he wrote:

> In the splendour of the post house, the grand official sits,
> Raining curses on underlings who are tardy in kneeling,
> One thousand, ten thousand, jostle to catch a glimpse.
> The road before His Excellency is surely churned to mud,
> As servants in gorgeous costumes stand proudly at attention.
> A ragged beggar comes forward watched closely by a spy.
> He fails to kneel and evokes the fury of His Lordship.
> How could a grand official know the beggar man is starving?

Later he spent nine years writing the drama *Peach Blossom Fan*, which rocked the capital with its exposé of vicious intriguing among the mandarins. It was widely copied by hand and performances of the play were completely sold out. When the Kangxi emperor learned of the play, he asked for the script and read it himself, and shortly afterwards dismissed Kong Shangren from office. Filled with indignation, Kong Shangren returned home to Qufu. Compared with Kong Jisu and Kong Jifen, he was fortunate in having a home to return to. He was later buried in the Forest of Confucius close to where my father's grave lies. Whenever we swept father's grave, we would always stand for a moment beside his as well.

Grandma Zhang, Our 'Honorary Relations'

Among the many friends and relations of our family there was one particular family who were neither scholars nor officials, but the descendants of honest farm people. The family, named Zhang, lived in Zhangyang Village near the Forest of Confucius and were presided over by an old woman whom everyone called Grandma Zhang. Each time there was a wedding or a funeral at the Kong Mansion, she would bring her entire family along to share in the feasting. The other guests were all noble aristocrats bedecked with glittering finery, but she came in simple peasant's garb of coarse material. Beside their elegant refinement she appeared plain and unsophisticated, yet she had more dignity than any of them. Although the servants were better dressed than she, they served her with the utmost care and she was highly respected by the whole Kong family.

Only some years later when I came to know the story of Kong Mo did I understand why Grandma Zhang came to the Kong Mansion with such spirit and self-assurance.

The forty-third generation descendant of Confucius, Kong Renyu, was an only son. When he was nine years old the country was thrown into turmoil by constant wars. The Kong Mansion was a long way from the court, emoluments were cut off and Kong Renyu's father lost his noble rank and had to make his living as a district magistrate. At the time there was a sweeper at the Mansion named Liu Mo who changed his name to Kong Mo on taking up service with the family. This was during the Later Tang dynasty (923–936), when all household servants had to change their surnames to Kong – only after the Ming dynasty was the rule reversed so that no servant was permitted to be named Kong. Kong Mo, determined to seize the peerage, murdered Renyu's father and, to eradicate all possible threats to his position, determined to murder the son. But by coincidence, the boy had gone to visit his nurse, Mother Zhang, and had not returned. When Kong Mo came to demand the boy, Mother Zhang dressed her own son, whose age and appearance resembled the child's, in Renyu's clothing; he was murdered in Renyu's place.

At the Kong Mansion, Kong Mo took possession of the great seal and tokens of authority, recommended himself for a peerage and passed himself off as a descendant of Confucius. In such turbulent times, the clan dared not speak out against him. Meanwhile, Kong Renyu lived with Mother Zhang as her son and after ten years of diligent study took part in the imperial examinations at the capital and was accepted into the Imperial College. From there he sent a memorial to the Mingzong emperor (reigned 926–934) exposing Kong Mo's misdeeds. Officials were sent to Qufu to investigate and Kong Mo was impeached and executed. Kong Renyu was permitted to return to the Kong Mansion to claim his peerage. Later generations gave him the honorific title of 'Restorer of the Clan', and after his death the Requite Ancestral Kindness Hall was built in his honour and a memorial tablet was erected in the Worship the Sage Chapel inside the Temple of Confucius.

To show his gratitude for Mother Zhang's care and protection, Kong Renyu petitioned the emperor to permit the Kong family to recognise the Zhang family as eternal honorary relatives. All descendants of the Zhang family would be received at the Kong Mansion as honoured guests and to contravene this rule would be a serious breach of family etiquette. From then on, Mother Zhang was called 'Grandma Zhang' by the whole clan and this became her official title. Kong Renyu presented Mother Zhang with a dragon-head walking stick with which she was to discipline the wife of the Yansheng Duke should she see fit. On her death her title and walking stick were inherited by the wife of her eldest son.

To commemorate Mother Zhang, a small wood near Zhangyang Village was renamed the Zhang Family Forest, and every Yansheng Duke erected a Requite Kindness Tablet to her memory in the Forest of Confucius. Each time sacrificial ceremonies to Kong Renyu were held, two direct descendants of the Zhang family would take part in the proceedings and the Zhang family would sometimes be entrusted with sweeping the ancestral graves in the Forest of Confucius.

The Qufu County Annals also record that one member of the Zhang family was admitted by imperial order into the Imperial Academy, but this is the only evidence to suggest it was so. I had never heard it mentioned and the family elders knew nothing of it either. I can only guess that being accustomed to working on the land, the Zhangs placed little value on the empty title and continued to farm for their livelihood. The dragon-headed walking stick

Kong Decheng (centre) with KMT dignitaries and foreign guests in the
Rear Flower Garden

Descendants of Confucius, Yan Hui, Mencius and Zengzi

Kong Decheng with his wife, Sun Qifang, and their son and daughter, Chongqing, 1945

The author at the Sixth National People's Political Consultative
Conference, May 1984

In front of the Kong Mansion. Left to right: her son, the author, her
daughter Ke Lan and her grandson

The author at Confucius' tomb, 1978

disappeared long ago, but the honorary relationship continued throughout the centuries.

The Grandma Zhang that I remember always came to the Mansion leaning on a walking stick. It was an ordinary walking stick and in fact she was hale and hearty, but perhaps she felt some symbolic need to carry it nonetheless. She was a fifty-year-old country woman in a coarse cloth jacket and loose trousers bound tightly around the ankles. Her feet were bound and she invariably carried a bamboo basket on her arm. She was not at all discomfited to find herself feasting alongside high officials and aristocrats, and talked and joked at the top of her voice. After eating and drinking her fill she would leave with her basket full of delicacies. Madame Tao, the Duchess, was always very respectful to Grandma Zhang in front of the guests. Several times I heard her quietly ordering the servants: 'Grandma Zhang has arrived, give her whatever she wants, and don't do anything to offend her.' I suspect that this was not so much done out of a sense of pious respect for the ancestors, as out of the desire to avoid a scene. I remember once a servant boy slighted Grandma Zhang and she stood outside the Great Hall, cursing him in a manner so loud and abrasive that a speechless hush fell over each and every bystander. I was still a young child and had never witnessed name-calling in public in my life – regardless of what anyone was thinking privately, everyone in the Mansion was always outwardly very polite and refined – so to me it was a novel experience and I remained transfixed at her side watching with great fascination.

Madame Tao had ordered that Grandma Zhang be given special treatment, but in fact Grandma would never ask for anything but steamed bread and wine. When the servant boys realised this they arranged for her to eat in the western room of the Qianshang Building. The western wing of the same courtyard contained the wine cellar and the kitchen where bread was steamed.

Grandma Zhang always brought a sizeable crowd with her – not only her whole family but virtually the whole village too. At Madame Tao's funeral Grandma Zhang's party occupied six tables of ten seats each. The numbers gradually decreased though, until at Decheng's wedding they occupied only two tables.

Half a century has passed but the memory of Grandma Zhang still stands out clear and fresh in my mind. Most of all I admire her lack of any sense of inferiority when mixing with aristocrats far above her own station. This was not because of the power symbolised by a long-lost dragon-headed cane, but because of her own dauntless spirit.

Sacrifices to Confucius

Deep within the Inner Apartments of the palatial Kong Mansion, I would wake at night to hear the lowing of cattle and the cries of sheep drifting faintly through the windows. These sounds were coming from the 'sacred kitchens' behind the Rear Hall in the Temple of Confucius where the butcher household, clad in red silk cloaks, were slaughtering beasts in preparation for the sacrificial offerings to Confucius.

The most important duty of the Kong Mansion was to offer sacrifices to Confucius. It was believed that solemn sacrifices to the sage and meticulous care in conducting funeral rites for one's parents had a great influence on the morals of the ordinary people. Each year the Kong Mansion held over fifty major and minor sacrificial ceremonies to Confucius. The most important were the four *Ding* Sacrifices held on the fourth day of the first month of each of the four seasons. In addition there were the four Secondary *Ding* Sacrifices held ten days after the *Ding* Sacrifices and the eight small sacrifices held on the Clear and Bright (*Qingming*) Festival (when ancestral graves were swept), the Dragon Boat Festival, the Mid-Autumn Festival, New Year's Eve, the first day of the sixth lunar month, the first day of the tenth lunar month, and the anniversaries of the birth and death of Confucius. Sacrifices were also offered on the first and fifteenth of each month and at each of the year's twenty-four solar terms.

The Kong Mansion had a special organisation for carrying out the sacrifices to Confucius. The Department of Music supervised the music and *Bayi* dance performed during ceremonies, took care of the musical instruments and dancers' ritual implements and undertook the training of all the performers. Sacrifices were presided over by the Yansheng Duke, with eighty masters of ceremonies and 103 other officials specialised in offering sacrifices, performing the rites, etc. There were also 120 (and sometimes 184) dancers with flags and musicians with bamboo flutes, drums, or *qin*. Major sacrificial ceremonies were also attended by students and teachers of the Four Clans Teachers College, members of the four clans and guests, bringing the total number of participants to over 1,000.

After my father died, and while my younger brother was still a baby, the clan chief took the place of the Yansheng Duke as the head of sacrificial ceremonies. When he reached the age of two or three, members of the household began to practise the rites with Decheng. They had endless patience, now coaxing, now encouraging while my elder sister and I stood at one side copying everything he was taught. At the age of five he formally took the leading role in sacrificial ceremonies. At the four *Ding* Sacrifices and the sacrifice to mark the birth of the sage, the ceremonies were particularly awe-inspiring. Besides the participants mentioned above, there were high government officials (all heads of central government departments or higher) and a host of reporters and other guests. Before this imposing crowd, five-year-old Decheng wearing ancient ceremonial robes took his place at the head of the assembly. In the course of the elaborate sacrificial ceremonies he had to walk a long way: from the front of the Apricot Altar he detoured to the Moon Terrace where he had to kowtow numerous times. He was very obedient and not in the least timid. Chen Jingrong and Wu Jianzhang walked on either side of him, and when Decheng found the steps of the Hall of Great Achievements too tall for his short legs, one of them would pick him up and carry him to the top in his arms.

Three days before major ceremonies, my brother would move to a study in the Temple of Confucius where he would bathe and rehearse the ceremonial rites. He would be carried into the Temple through the main gate in a gold-roofed sedan chair borne by eight chair-bearers. During this period of preparation, he was not permitted to leave by the Main Gate, but there was a small door in the wall dividing the Temple and the Mansion which he could use to visit his family. This was officially known as 'entering openly and leaving secretly'. We often used the door to visit Decheng too.

There were many people involved in practising the rites; musicians and dancers, masters of ceremonies, sacrificial attendants and so on. Specially rigorous demands were made on the master of ceremonies who opened the proceedings. His voice had to be loud and clear, for he stood at one side of the terrace before the Hall of

Great Achievements and shouted commands for each event of the ceremony to commence. According to the regulations, his voice had to be loud enough to be heard throughout the whole town of Qufu. The official who performed this duty went to the small copse inside the Temple of Confucius every day to train his voice, increasing his practice-time as the ceremonies drew near. His voice was not only loud and clear, but had a rich musical quality, and as in reciting poetry, he drew out the ends of words, rather like the spoken parts in modern Beijing opera.

The Yinzan official stood alongside lantern bearers, censer bearers and attendants next to the Yansheng Duke and guided him through each step of the ceremony. The sacrifice to Confucius began with a kowtow before the Apricot Altar, after which the procession circled round to the terrace in front of the Hall of Great Achievements and mounted the steps. The lantern and censer bearers had to remain outside the door, but attendants were admitted.

Inside the Hall of Great Achievements the master of sacrifices knelt in obeisance before a statue of Confucius. On either side were ranged statues of Confucius' 'four followers' – Yan Hui, Zengzi, Mencius and Kong Ji, the grandson of the sage, together with twelve statues of Confucius' best known disciples including Zi Lu, Zi Gong and Min Ziqian, the Song neo-Confucianist Zhu Xi etc. To the right and left of the hall were the green-tiled, red-pillared east and west wings containing statues of famous historical Confucian scholars such as the philosophers Dong Zhongshu of the Han dynasty, Han Yu of the Tang dynasty and Wang Shouren of the Ming dynasty, known collectively as the 'later sages' or 'later Confucianists'.[1] As the master of sacrifices knelt before the image of Confucius, lesser officials simultaneously knelt before each of the other statues and performed the same rituals. Inside the Hall of Great Achievements,

---

[1] Yan Hui and Zengzi were disciples of Confucius; Mencius (*c.* 370–290 BC), a follower of Confucius' ideas, considered himself a mere transmitter of the sage's thoughts but his view, that man is by nature good, became one of the fundamental tenets of Confucianism. The other philosophers commemorated in the hall are later interpreters of Confucianism, most notably Han Yu, the ninth century essayist and critic of Buddhism, whose ideas anticipated those of the great neo-Confucian, Zhu Xi (AD 1130–1200), whose commentaries and re-examination of Confucianism led to the greater stress on the stability of the family and the state as a family.

scores of ancient musical instruments – bells, chime-stones, drums, pan-pipes and porcelain ocarinas were laid out beside ancient sacrificial vessels – wine pitchers, meat containers, lamps, wine cups etc. Sacrificial offerings included whole cattle, pigs and sheep, salt, cat's blood, lotus-seed cakes and water-chestnuts. White sandal-wood incense was burnt while eight rows of dancers clad in ancient costumes swayed to and fro in time to the music. My brother's costume was a tunic of dark magenta with wide bell sleeves embroidered with flowers, worn with a skirt-like garment. The sacrificial ceremony began at midnight and lasted for about an hour. Procedures went as follows:

Masters of Ceremonies (M.C.): Musicians and dancers take your places. Officers, tend to your duties. Sacrificial assistants, take your places. Sacrifice stewards, take your places.

Yinzan Official (Y.Z.): Everyone is ready.

M.C.: Offer the sacrifice of feathers and blood.

Y.Z.: Wash the hands in the wash basin, go to the wine vessel and offer libations. Kneel and sprinkle the wine on the ground, kowtow three times.

M.C.: Receive the spirit.

(*music*) Begin the Manifesting Harmony Movement to receive the spirit.

Y.Z.: Wash the hands. Ascend the hall and kneel before the statue of the Divine First Teacher, kowtow. Stand erect, offer incense and then return to your position.

M.C.: Kneel three times, kowtowing each time. Make the offering of silk, carry out the initial offering rites.

(*music*) Begin the Proclaim Harmony Movement to mark the initial offering rites.

Y.Z.: Wash the hands. Wash the wine pitcher. Move to the wine jar. Responsible official, remove the cloth cover and fill the pitcher. Go before the Sagely Divine First Teacher and kowtow. Stand erect and make the offering of wine. Return to your position.

M.C.: Carry out the rites to conclude the offerings.

(*music*) Begin the Describing Harmony Movement to mark the completion of offerings.

Y.Z.: Wash the hands. Wash the wine pitcher. Move to the wine jar. Responsible official, remove the cloth cover and fill the pitcher.

Go before the Sagely Divine First Teacher and kowtow, stand erect and present the offering of wine.

M.C.: Bestow the blessed sacrificial meat.

Y.Z. (*Official with meat*): Ascend to the hall. Both officials, take up the correct position. Present the wine. Receive the blessed sacrificial meat. Kneel once and kowtow three times, return to your positions.

M.C.: Kneel three times with nine kowtows. Bury the offerings of food.

(*music*) Begin the Beautiful Peace Movement to mark the offering of food.

M.C.: Bid farewell to the spirits.

(*music*) Begin the Peace of Moral Virtue Movement to bid farewell to the spirits.

M.C.: Kneel three times, kowtow nine times. Hold the longevity cloth [symbolising the wish for long life] proffered in the hands, take up the position for burning the offering.

Y.Z.: Go before the tablet of the late Sagely King. Burn the longevity cloth. Pray for him. Return to your position.

M.C.: Here end the rites.

The longevity cloths used in sacrifices were silks and cottons placed in a paper basket and called 'cowries' (implying something of value, as cowrie-shells were an ancient form of currency). At the end of the ceremony they were taken to the Burn the Shells Temple behind the Hall of Great Achievements and burnt by the Master of Sacrifices.

The Master of Sacrifices frequently washed his hands. This was in compliance with the clan rule which stated that sacrificial ceremonies 'must be abundant, clean, sincere and conducted respectfully'. In addition, one of the Qing emperors issued an imperial edict ordering that 'sacrificial ceremonies in the Temple of Confucius and Forest of Confucius must be carried out with meticulous attention to cleanliness.' The slightest act of neglect would be considered deeply disrespectful to the ancestors.

By the time my brother Decheng was ten, he was quite familiar with the rituals of sacrifice to Confucius. He walked with a solemn step and kept his eyes raised instead of watching the ground. With each pace his feet would land neatly in the centre of one of the square flagstones on his path. The old people all praised his celestial bearing, but he himself was indifferent to such praise and I didn't appreciate it either; we were far more interested in galloping on our bamboo hobby-horses through the Rear Flower Garden, or flying kites.

Under the rule of Chiang Kai-shek, the Nationalist Government sent the Head of the Central Ministry of Propaganda, Chu Minyi, to perform sacrifices to Confucius, and the Chairman of Shandong Province, Han Fuju, also came several times. They didn't bring the texts of the ceremonies with them, but in order to show the seriousness of their intentions had them sent to Qufu separately. Han Fuju was a rough, uncultured man incapable of making the usual laudatory speeches about 'the moral path that has excelled from the ancient past to the present day; virtue that shines in China and abroad', and during the New Life Movement (launched by Chiang Kai-shek in 1934) which promoted traditional morals and the revival of Confucianism, he remarked in a speech at the Mansion: 'Confucius is in luck again today.' The listening clan members weren't sure whether to laugh or feel annoyed.

The celebration of Confucius' birthday held in August 1934 during the New Life Movement, was the most majestic ceremony during the entire period of Chiang Kai-shek's rule. The central government sent Ye Chucang, a top official, as representative, accompanied by scores of lesser officials. Over 1,000 other guests also came and were housed in the Kong Mansion and the Twelve Mansions, all of which were filled to capacity. The Kong Mansion had to hurriedly organise a large group of servants to provide bedding for all the visitors.

Sacrifices to Confucius conducted by central government representatives were called National Sacrifices, while those presided over by my little brother Decheng were called Family Sacrifices. The two ceremonies differed in a number of ways. No offerings were made at the National Sacrifices, but a floral wreath was presented by the government representative. Ye Chucang had an exquisite wreath of lily magnolias transported specially from Nanjing for the occasion.

At the National Sacrifices, ancient costumes were replaced by long gowns and mandarin jackets worn with a long sash across the chest. There was a rule that no one in street clothing was permitted to enter the Temple of Confucius, but many reporters and guests, not aware of this, came without long gowns. After arriving in Qufu they were obliged to borrow the proper gowns from wherever they could, and there was temporarily a serious shortage of long gowns in the town. The kowtow was also dispensed with in favour of a formal bow and the time of the ceremony was changed from midnight to seven in the morning. The rituals proceeded as follows:

1. The ceremony commences.
2. The body of worshippers stands in solemn respect.
3. The Master of Sacrifices takes up position.
4. Other participants take their positions.
5. Sacrificial assistants take their positions.
6. Incense is offered.
7. The floral wreath is presented.
8. The wine pitcher is presented.
9. The sacrificial oration is read.
10. The assembled worshippers bow three times to the first Teacher Confucius.
11. Conclusion.

Following the National Sacrifices in the morning, a second ceremony was held in the afternoon before the sage's tomb in the Forest of Confucius. This was followed at midnight by a family ceremony in which the government officials took no part, but merely watched from the side. On the completion of all the ceremonies, the sacrificial meat was divided among the participants and the Twelve Mansions. Everyone received a small slice.

Sacrificial ceremonies were very expensive. Before each ceremony, the Kong Mansion would have to sell large amounts of its grain reserves to meet the enormous costs. According to statistics, about 16,000 dollars were spent on sacrificial ceremonies in the Temple and Forest of Confucius in the year 1928.

According to the rules of the Kong Mansion, no women were allowed to take part in sacrificial ceremonies. The participation of women would have been an insult to the ancestors and besides, it was believed that with a woman on the scene, none of the musical instruments in the Temple of Confucius would produce a sound. It was said that once during a sacrifice to Confucius the musical bells suddenly stopped sounding. Investigation revealed a Buddhist nun among the crowd of onlookers. Only when she had been thrown out did the bells sound again. I don't know who made up this story, but it was probably fabricated in order to verify the statement by Confucius that, 'Women and inferior men are difficult to handle.' But after the founding of the Republic, these regulations were relaxed. As young ladies of the Kong Mansion, my sister and I often watched ceremonies from the side with no interference. Some of the girls from the Twelve Mansions used to come and watch too.

But in the Annals of Qufu, there is mention of a woman taking part in sacrifices to Confucius, playing the exalted role of Master of Sacrifices. This unique figure was the sister of the Yuan dynasty Dade emperor (reigned 1295–1308) who came twice to Qufu to sacrifice to Confucius after the fiftieth generation descendant had completed renovating the Hall of Great Achievements. An inscribed stele was erected to mark the occasion.

Funeral Ceremonies

The proper conduct of the funeral ceremonies of one's parents was one of the basic rules of the Kong family, and was also the criterion by which the moral standards of Confucius' descendants were measured. Each of the mansions had to keep its own vast wardrobe of mourning apparel, as a different costume was worn depending on one's relationship to the deceased.

The Kong Mansion practised some unique funeral rituals. As friends and relatives arrived to participate in the funeral, a band in a marquee before the gate would begin to play. One tune would greet the arrival of male guests, a second tune would welcome female guests, and a third tune would greet men and women arriving together. On either side of the gate stood the door gods *Fangbi* and *Fangxiang*, two huge figures about twenty feet high constructed of silk stretched on wooden frames. Their costumes and facial make-up were very similar to those of characters from the Beijing Opera. A person would stand inside each figure and look out through the navel, manipulating it in such a way that the figure could walk and perform various other movements. When the music began on the arrival of guests, the great figures would move forward to receive them. *Fangbi* and *Fangxiang* would also lead the funeral procession, preceding the coffin and mourners to the side of the tomb where their presence repelled evil influences from the grave.

These door gods were the exclusive property of the Kong Mansion, and the Twelve Mansions were not permitted to use them. The men who manipulated the huge puppets were always rewarded handsomely for their services.

The shrouding of the body consisted of dressing and encoffining. From the third to the fifth day after death, the body would be dressed in ordinary clothes; after this, these were changed for a burial costume and the body was placed in a coffin. Women were dressed in a phoenix coronet and an embroidered official cape. A pearl was placed inside the mouth and the body was sprinkled with perfume. After this, the entire corpse, including the face, was wrapped tightly in three layers of silk – the two inner layers green for women and red for men, with the third and outermost layer of white silk. The close, tight wrapping produced an object resembling a large white flower vase. In the Twelve Mansions, the dead were also shrouded in this way.

There were specific rules governing the temporary sheltering of coffins before burial.

The coffins of the Yansheng Duke and his wife rested in the Qianshang Building of the Inner Apartments while concubines and relatives living at the Mansion rested in the White Tiger Hall. The Black Dragon Hall and White Tiger Hall were built to the front and rear of the Mansion. According to tradition, children should be born in the Black Dragon Hall and deaths should occur in the White Tiger Hall, as this was propitious according to the *fengshui* of the Kong Mansion. But few close relatives lived at the Mansion and I don't remember the White Tiger Hall ever being used for its designated purpose. My mother's bier was not placed there but in the Western College.

The bier shelter was covered with a blue glass roof under which were placed paper figures (representing servants), paper horses and a bowl of treasures, a money tree, and gold and silver shoe-shaped ingots, all of paper, which were burnt so as to accompany the departing soul to the afterworld. In addition there were hundreds of burial objects for use in the afterlife: small tin teapots and tea dishes, small wooden tables and chairs, a bed complete with bedding and embroidered clothing and shoes, all functional miniatures less than two centimetres in length. They were so exquisitely made that even the tiny pointed shoes were intricately embroidered with complicated designs. One of my aunts, Madame Yuan, was famous for the burial objects she made. The patterns that she embroidered had to be viewed through a magnifying glass to be seen clearly. All these burial objects were placed in the tomb at the time of burial.

The bier under the blue glass roof was concealed behind a large red silk curtain on which was written the full official title of the deceased. The curtain was draped over the coffin when the funeral procession began.

The number of pall-bearers varied according to the status of the deceased. Residents of the Kong Mansion were permitted sixty-four pall-bearers while those of the Twelve Mansions were only entitled to thirty-two.

Another Kong clan regulation governing both the Kong Mansion and the Twelve Mansions stipulated that upon the death of a parent, one could neither receive guests, listen to music, nor attend operas for a period of three years. During this mourning period Kong Mansion officials still received their provisions and funds as usual, but government officials did not. As a child I was taught the importance of this observance: Confucius, they said, had a disciple called Zai Yu who believed that three years of mourning was too long and so proposed reducing it. Confucius strongly censured him: 'Zai Yu is not benevolent. Only at the age of three could he leave the bosom of his parents. Did he not receive three years of love from his parents?' According to Confucius, three years of mourning was the absolute minimum that one's conscience should allow. In the course of my rudimentary education, the importance of this was stressed repeatedly.

No deaths at the Mansion were overlooked and even the death of an errand boy was marked by despatching a representative – usually a high-ranking servant – to attend the funeral. This representative was known as the 'Heavenly Envoy' and had the full powers and rights of the Yansheng Duke, the only difference being that he was carried in a green sedan chair with a silver roof and four chair bearers instead of the Duke's red, gold-roofed chair with eight bearers. Preceding him was the Duke's honour guard including men carrying poles topped with over a hundred different symbols of authority – golden melons, battle axes, 'Heaven-Facing Stools' (resembling inverted stirrups), banners, gongs, parasols, fans, and signs reading 'Silence!' and 'Make way!' As if receiving the emperor, the whole family of the deceased would kneel in welcome at the side of the road outside their village.

According to clan regulations, if an errand runner died inside the Kong Mansion he could not be carried out through the gate, but had to be lifted out over the walls. As the walls of the Kong Mansion were very high, it was fortunate that no errand boys were known to have died inside them in the past, for the task of hauling the coffin out over the walls would have presented enormous difficulties. When I lived at the Kong Mansion, this regulation had already fallen into disuse. An errand runner called Zhao Anfu who died in the Mansion was carried out through the gate without anyone raising objections, and Madame Tao, who was the highest author-ity in the Mansion at the time, pretended to ignore the regulation and allowed the incident to pass.

To the east of the Main Gate of the Mansion was a small alley known as 'Ghost Lane'. Because the funeral processions of ordinary people were not permitted to pass before the Main Gate of the Kong Mansion, they had to make a detour through Ghost Lane to the burial ground. Apart from these funeral processions, few people ever used the alley.

The Forest of Confucius had been the cemetery of the Kong clan for over 2,000 years. It was filled with countless tombs and stone tablets, the most carefully kept being those of the first and last three generations. The first three generations were Confucius, his son Kong Li and his grandson Kong Ji, while the last three generations were my father Kong Lingyi, his father Kong Xiangke and his grandfather Kong Fanhao. The busiest time at the Forest was during the Clear and Bright (*Qingming*) Festival when the gateways were thronged with people all day long. At that time, the 'Forest Gate Fair', a huge country market similar to the temple fairs in traditional China, was held outside the cemetery gates.

But the Clear and Bright Festival was not the only occasion for a visit to the Forest of Confucius. Frequently we went to offer sacrifices to my father, grandfather, great-grandfather and even great-great-grandfather and their relatives. Sacrifices were offered on their birthdays, the anniversaries of their deaths, the anniversary of the birth of Confucius, the Clear and Bright Festival, the first day of the tenth lunar month and on many other fixed dates. Besides this we also had to worship at the Family Temple, the Worship the Shadows Hall, the Hall for Cherishing Ancestral Kindness, and the Requite Ancestral Kindness Hall. The sacrificial rites were extremely elaborate and formed a large part of daily life. There was a huge, thick book inside the manager's office which recorded the dates of the births and deaths of clan members, a wooden board was hung up in front of the Great Hall and at the beginning of each month a list of the dates, places (Temple or Forest of Confucius) and names of those to be worshipped in the coming month were posted. It was rather like a list of homework assignments and we conscientiously went in accordance with this table, kowtowing and offering sacrifices as required.

The party that accompanied us to sweep the graves consisted of over a hundred people. Members of the Sacrifice Carriers Household carried our huge, square sacrificial chests filled with layer upon layer of offerings on sacrificial plates. There were cakes made from lotus-seed flour, steamed bread, meat and wine, and sandalwood incense to be burnt on red-hot rounds of charcoal. There were also servants carrying burners for making tea, as well as the security troops and various other attendants.

Before sweeping the graves, we always stopped to rest at the Pavilion for Changing Clothes just beyond the Zhushui River Bridge, and after the sweeping, we children would rush off and play in the Forest. In the tall grass to the south-west of Confucius' tomb, there was a slanting cave which was narrow at the mouth but which broadened inside. The servants and old nurses, who wouldn't allow us to go near it for fear of us falling in, told us the story behind it. The cave was called the Oil Basket Tomb or Cattle Pen Grave and was a relic of the Qin dynasty (221–206 BC). At the time, old people who lived past the age of sixty were buried alive. Filial sons were naturally loathe to treat their parents in this way, so they dug 'oil basket tombs' for the old people to live in. Each night they would lower food and drink to them in bamboo baskets. Many such tombs were used by the Kong clan at the time.

The *fengshui* of the Forest of Confucius was an extremely important concern, for in feudal times it was believed to be closely linked to the destiny of the nation. In an audience with my great-great-grandfather, Kong Qingrong, one of the Qing emperors instructed him:

> In the Forest of Confucius meticulous attention must be paid to *fengshui*. You must make absolutely sure that you refuse even the smallest changes [in the layout of the Forest]. Our dynasty rules the empire by dint of cultural eminence and its fate is bound to the *fengshui* of the Forest of Confucius, so you must not allow the least negligence.

In 1904, the thirtieth year of the reign of the Guangxu emperor, surveying was being carried out for the Tianjin-Pukou Railway. According to the original plans, it was to run south from Xiemating and pass through Qufu at a point close to the western wall of the Forest of Confucius. My father was highly disturbed by this news and sent several memorials to the throne saying that the railway would 'shake the tomb of the sage,' 'stop the sage's very pulse,' and that 'the spirits of the ancestors would not be able to rest in peace.' Finally the plans were altered and the line was built with a great curve around Qufu. One of my elderly relatives once said to me, 'The reason why this family of ours has not declined in a thousand years is because our *fengshui* is so good. The tombs of the emperors lie on a north-south axis, so their descendants can only remain aristocrats for the course of one dynasty; but Confucius' grave is slightly off the north-south axis, so his sons and grandsons are protected for all time.'

Just why Confucius' misaligned tomb should have protected his descendants she didn't make clear. Afterwards I went to the Forest of Confucius and carefully examined the sage's tomb: it was nothing more than a little round hillock and I really couldn't tell whether it was off-centre or not.

Ordinary anniversaries of the births and deaths of the ancestors were celebrated only by the household concerned, who sacrificed in their own family temple or swept the graves in the Forest of Confucius. But each time an important 'deathday' was celebrated (fiftieth, sixtieth, seventieth, etc.), the whole family would gather for 'nether-world longevity celebrations', which were just as lively as birthday celebrations for the living. A large portrait of the deceased was hung inside a hall and the whole family, dressed in their best with the women in bright red skirts, would kowtow before it and wish it long life. The most ceremonious occasion I remember was a celebration for my grandmother, Madame Peng, held when I was a child of seven or eight. These were held in the Hall of Loyalty and Forbearance, where grandmother's portrait was hung surrounded by longevity silks presented by various members of the family. In the courtyard, an orchestra in a marquee played soothing music. Peaches symbolising longevity and three-legged, silver wine-goblets were placed on a scarlet offerings-table that stood before the portrait. Relatives coming to offer birthday felicitations would fill a goblet with wine, raise it to the portrait and then pour it on the ground. The wine was thus 'drunk' by the departed spirit.

5

Times Of Turmoil

Poverty

From the early 1920s to the late 30s, the Kong Mansion economy was all expenditure and no income, and one major feature of the household was its imminent financial collapse.

With the founding of the Republic and the downfall of the dynastic system in 1911 the Duke's annual stipend was cut off and imperial gifts no longer flowed into the Mansion. The system of selling official posts was also abolished, leaving the family with no cash income whatsoever and totally reliant on payments in kind made by peasants renting land – payments which were virtually impossible to collect.

This is no exaggeration: the degree to which the Kong Mansion had sunk into poverty is difficult to believe. The accountant's office was frequently without a cent and sometimes when visitors came, couldn't provide the money to purchase two ounces of wine – the servant sent out to buy it had to pay from his own pocket.

There were many reasons why we didn't receive rent: natural disasters, wars, the anti-Confucian movement, official corruption, and disorderly land administration.

The land belonging to the Kong Mansion was spread over more than thirty counties in five provinces. All of it was sacrificial fields – imperial gifts intended to provide income for the family to continue sacrificing to the ancestors. But the amount and type of land varied with each dynasty, and the rules governing rent payments became highly confused. There were several different types of tenants: those who had been working the land when it was presented to the family; those who had been taken on afterwards and had to contribute more corvée labour than the first category; and a third category who did no corvée labour, but had to pay higher rent. According to

regulations, the Kong Mansion was not permitted to sell its sacrificial fields, so tenants who wished to farm them had to pay two
dollars (enough to buy twenty kilos of wheat flour) for a leasing
permit. But by the time of the Republic, the situation had become
very confused, and land administration officials – from those who
worked in the Kong Mansion offices to the general collectors and
village rent collectors – all sold land secretly to line their own
pockets. Tenants also sublet their land at a profit. So much land was
lost that the records of tenants and land in the land administration
office's 'red book' bore little resemblance to the real situation, and
in several places fierce disputes arose over land ownership. But this
confusion had already existed before the Republic; long standing
historical problems became rapidly worse under the new regime.

During the reign of the Guangxu emperor (1875–1908), the
Provincial Governor Zhang Yao submitted a memorial to the
throne saying that there were vast numbers of dry fields in Tongshan and Pei counties that should have come under the jurisdiction
of the Kong Mansion, and asking the court to investigate the
situation and re-allocate land to compensate the Mansion. The
court assigned Zhang Zhidong to investigate, but he found it
impossible to settle the correct distribution of land. The following
conclusion was reached: 'The lost sacrificial fields cannot be traced;
therefore 2,350 acres of land in the Tongshan and Pei counties will
be re-allocated to the Kong Mansion and the Xuzhou District shall
remit 2,890 strings of cash per year in rent.' This rent paid to the
Kong Mansion by the Xuzhou District was cut off in the third year
of the Republic (1914). In 1926, the Governor of Shandong Province wrote to the provincial Department of Finance requesting that
6,600 acres of lost sacrificial fields in Huangtugang be restored to
the Kong Mansion. But because of the civil turmoil at the time, the
files were lost and the land was not returned. In 1934, Chiang
Kai-shek had Jia Muyi establish a Central Committee for Rectifying
the Distribution of Sacrificial Fields to identify the remaining
sacrificial fields. After three years they were still unable to come to
any clear conclusions. When the Anti-Japanese War broke out, the
task was abandoned.

Two progressive educators, Cai Yuanpei and Jiang Menglin,
both former chancellors of Beijing University and Ministers of
Education under the Kuomintang government, appealed to Chiang

Kai-shek to abolish the whole sacrificial field system. Intervention by Kong Xiangxi (H. H. Kung[1]) prevented their demands being realised, but their influence was still very powerful – not only did distant provinces such as Henan and Anhui refuse to pay their rent, but the dissension gradually spread until tenants in the Sishui region near Qufu also refused to pay. Many villages paid no rent for seven or eight years. In numerous cases, the tenants did pay rent, but it was all embezzled by corrupt land-administration officials who made false reports to the Mansion claiming they had collected nothing. I remember one land administration official called Shang Shandao, a tall, heavily built man with an honest air. Several members of the clan jointly reported to Kong Xiangxi that he bullied tenants and cheated the Kong Mansion; he refused to reduce the rent in years of natural disasters and peasants were fined for late payments. Furthermore, every cent he collected ended up in his own purse. He was dismissed from his post, but I subsequently learned that those who turned him in were no better, his exposure was just a case of 'dog eat dog'.

In the past, private donations were an important source of Kong Mansion revenue and many construction projects were financed in this way. When my father was alive, a Hong Kong merchant named Guo Zhanxiang donated 40,000 silver dollars to build a Temple of the Sage on Ni Mountain. The Rear Hall in the Temple of Confucius was built with 20,000 silver dollars donated by Zhang Zongchang and the Temple and Forest were renovated with money contributed by Sun Duoyan of Anhui Province. In addition, many people donated small sums of money. Originally, the money went directly to the Kong Mansion to cover expenses, but after the war between Chiang Kai-shek on one side, and Yan Xishan and Feng Yuxiang[2]

---

[1] H. H. Kung (1881–1967) was a Western-educated banker and businessman who was a major figure in the Kuomintang government between 1928 and 1945. A friend and in-law of both Sun Yat-sen and Chiang Kai-shek, he belonged to a Shanxi branch of the Kong clan and considered himself a descendant of the sage. For this reason, he took a special interest in the welfare of the Mansion and the fortunes of the Kong estate.

[2] See note p. 75. Two northern 'warlords' or regional military rulers. With the collapse of the Qing dynasty, the Nationalist (Kuomintang) government failed to gain complete control of China but had to accommodate local warlords or take them on in battle.

on the other, devastated the Mansion, Temple and Forest, contributions to restore the home of the sage were handled by Han Fuju; who appropriated most of the money for his own personal use. When he was about to leave Jinan, he packed the money into boxes marked 'medicine' and shipped it out on an express train.

The Kong Mansion had no income, but it was impossible to reduce its expenditure. Not one of its hundreds of servants was dismissed; sacrifices were made as before; and there was also the cost of a Manifest Virtue Middle School, opened by the Central Education Department, but funded by the Kong Mansion. In those years the school staff often went for three or four months without pay. There was a primary school in Dong Village near Qufu which applied to the Kong Mansion for contributions to build a Confucian Temple in the village. For fear of losing face, the Mansion pledged fifty dollars – a meagre enough sum – but it was still unable to make the payment. The primary school pressed several times for the promised contribution, but the Kong Mansion wrote in reply: 'We acknowledge our commitment to contribute fifty dollars. This sum would have long since been forwarded were it not for economic difficulties at the Mansion. We hope you will permit us to temporarily postpone payment.' In the end, the money was never donated.

At that time, the Kong Mansion's sole method of solving its economic problems was to borrow money. On the one hand it was borrowed from Kong Xiangxi, Zhang Zongchang and Han Fuju, and on the other it came from the Mansion servants. Money was not only borrowed for large expenditures at the Mansion, it also had to be borrowed for little things like buying an oil lamp cover or a glass of wine. Almost all the servants with any relationship to the Inner Apartments lent money to the Mansion, and important, high-ranking servants such as Chen Jingrong, Zhao Yukun, Zhao Ankun and Liu Mengying were even more frequently sought out for loans. The Kong Mansion also had a small amount of privately owned land that was originally intended to be divided among the brothers of the Yansheng Duke when they left home. There were a few dozen acres scattered throughout the Qufu area, but they had all been mortgaged out.

In this poverty-stricken aristocratic house, the man who found life most difficult was Kong Yinqiu. After my father's death, my uncle Kong Lingyu took over management of the Mansion. When I was eleven, my uncle died and Kong Yinqiu was asked to take over the task. We called him Third Grandfather. It was his main job to devise ways of borrowing money, and especially at New Years, his job became every unpleasant. There was a saying at the Mansion: 'When the "pole facing heaven" is erected, creditors suddenly turn hostile.' Once the pole was erected on the twenty-eighth day of the twelfth lunar month of the year, debt collectors lined up at the entrance of the Kong Mansion from the Main Gate to the gate of the Inner Apartments, and it fell to Kong Yinqiu to try to put them off. When persuasion failed, the only choice was to borrow more money. In his letters, Kong described the bitter experience of being hounded for debts: 'I have borrowed 3,000 dollars from the Maowu Studio and another 300 from the Mingyue Pavilion. I am being pressed for both capital and interest. In the past month, there has not been a single day when they did not come demanding payment.' In a letter to her brother, Madame Tao, discussing preparing a dowry for my elder sister Deqi, wrote: 'I must have 3,000 dollars for the dowry. This has become a constant source of anxiety to me.' In fact, compared with traditional dowries provided by the Kong Mansion, this was a miserable enough sum. In 1933, in a letter to Feng Shu, she wrote:

> This spring I have urged that rents be paid promptly, but the collection is not going smoothly. This has led to an immediate drop in our income at a time when we are having difficulty meeting day-to-day expenses. New Year is coming, and expenses will be even greater.

In those years, when the family at the Kong Mansion met with relatives and friends, the conversation would always turn to such problems.

When we in the Inner Apartments learned of a debt collector at the door, the old maidservants would heave long sighs. They could tell us from first-hand experience how different the Kong Mansion was now from the old days. When my grandmother was alive, the Kong Mansion was occasionally itself short of money and had to pawn jewellery for ready cash. My grandmother would have one of her jewellery cases brought to the Inner Apartments from a storeroom, and then in the middle of the night direct a few trusted maidservants to remove some, replace it with bricks, and relock the case. In this way no one weighing the box could detect that anything was missing. The jewellery would then be pawned, and when redeemed, it would be quietly returned to its case. There was none of the open mortgaging of land that went on in later days, nor did debt collectors dare show their faces at the gate. Recalling the respect the Kong Mansion once commanded, the old maidservants related the following tale:

In the early years of the Republic, when my grandmother Madame Peng was still alive, the Kong Mansion ran short of money and arranged to borrow silver dollars from the Shandong Provincial Government. A small fleet of wheel-barrows was sent to fetch it, protected by a selected escort of burly bodyguards proficient in the martial arts. At the time, bandits ran rife throughout the area, and on the return journey, the escort was attacked by a notorious band of local brigands. After a fierce battle, the silver was carried off and the escort returned home in a sorry state. This loss came as a severe blow to the Kong Mansion, but a few days later a band of our own burly fellow-provincials suddenly appeared in town each pushing a wheelbarrow heaped with silver dollars. They were the same band of robbers who had stolen the silver in the first place. When they discovered that their booty belonged to the Kong Mansion, they decided it was wrong to steal money from the family of the sage and returned it intact to the Mansion. When the robbers arrived at the Main Gate, the inhabitants of the Mansion were too terrified to venture outside. The bandits made no attempt to enter the gate either, but just waited patiently in the street. When the news circulated that a band of brigands was returning money to the Mansion, practically the whole town came to watch the extra-ordinary sight.

But during my childhood, the standing of the Kong Mansion plunged along with its finances. During the Qing dynasty, the county magistrate was appointed by the Yansheng Duke and made judicial decisions in accordance with the Duke's instructions. When the county magistrate came to the Kong Mansion on business, he was not permitted to enter the second gate but had to wait outside. At Kong Mansion funerals, he was obliged to come and act as gatekeeper. But these conventions had all disappeared by the time I was born. There was a county magistrate called Song Wenchuan who often visited us at the Kong Mansion. He was not considered an important guest, and used to practise calligraphy with Decheng and tell him jokes. When his term of office ended he still visited the Mansion frequently. After the Anti-Japanese War, when Decheng and I were living in Nanjing, Song Wenchuan came to Nanjing from Qufu. He was unemployed and stayed as a non-paying guest.

Before the Anti-Japanese War, the Kong Mansion had already lost much of its political influence. At the time, this 'First Family Under Heaven' was already largely ignored, either deliberately or unwittingly, by the local government organs. For example, during the rule of the Northern Warlords and Chiang Kai-shek, the Temple to the Jade Emperor, the Temple to the God of War, the Temple to the Goddess of Mercy and the Temple to the God of the Profound Heavens at Dazhuang – all run under the patronage of the Kong Mansion – were demolished without the consent of the Mansion to provide building materials for other projects. One of the heads of the county Education Department occupied fifty acres of sacrificial fields and over three acres of Temple fields outside the town of Qufu. Once when a carriage belonging to the Mansion was travelling outside, it was highjacked by soldiers of the 72nd Division stationed in the area. The Kong Mansion had no choice but to contact their aide-de-camp and demand it back. At the time there were many mercenary soldiers about in the countryside who had no concept of 'venerating the sage' and would sometimes come leaping over our back wall into the Rear Flower Garden and steal whatever they could find. The Mansion often made formal protests to the 72nd Division in the name of my brother Decheng over events like these.

The Kong Mansion was poor, but compared to the neighbouring family of descendants of Yan Hui, it was quite well off. The Yan family were all bookworms, and in such financial straits they had to borrow grain in order to have enough to eat. The Kong Mansion was never short of grain, and at each birthday or festival at least a few guests were invited to the celebrations. But these banquets could not compare with those of the past when a birthday would be celebrated with a banquet for several thousand guests. On one occasion when my aunt, who looked after the Inner Apartments after Madame Tao's death (and was thus also mistress of the Kong Mansion), celebrated her birthday, she only invited a few women relatives. That day I wrote in my diary 'To wish Aunt a long life, we invited my Eldest Aunt, Fourth Aunt, Seventh Aunt, Ninth Aunt, Tenth Aunt and Eleventh Aunt to celebrate along with my elder sister and younger brother.' This reveals the scale of birthday celebrations held at that time.

Once Madame Tao decided to fell trees in the Forest of Confucius to sell as timber. Many precious trees were cut down, but no market was found for them, so they remained piled in the Forest. Another time, Madame Tao raised the possibility of selling the Duke's Mansion in Beijing, but this never happened. I heard that members of the clan opposed the idea on the grounds that ancestral property should not be touched.

The poverty of the Kong Mansion had one notable characteristic. There was an old saying: 'Even if a centipede dies, it never goes stiff' – an aristocratic family like the Kong Mansion that had known a thousand years of prosperity owned countless reserves of gold, silver and other precious materials, and although poor was not in utter destitution. I learned that many years later, when the Houtang Building which had stood empty for years was being swept clean of a thick layer of pigeon excrement, gold and pearls were found scattered on the floor buried under the filth. But when there was no money for a lamp cover or a glass of wine, no one ever considered solving the problem by sweeping the floor in the hope of finding some stray treasure. And as for the timeless antiques and priceless treasures that filled the Mansion – under no circumstances would anyone dream of touching, let alone selling, a single one.

The Storm Over *Confucius Meets Duchess Nanzi*

Opposite the Main Gate of the Kong Mansion stood the Shandong Province Second Teachers' College, now renamed the Qufu Teachers' College. In the early stages of the May 4th Movement, the slogan 'Down with the Confucian Curiosity Shop' was raised, and under the influence of progressive ideology, the students of the Second Teachers' College organised demonstrations, spread propaganda through the countryside and agitated against their dean, Kong Xiangtong, until he was forced to resign. In 1922, Wang Jinmei, the Communist Party member in charge of activities in the region, sent representatives to begin organising at the college and later sent Zhang Guancheng, Yang Yinhong and others to establish the Second Teachers' College's first Party branch. At the time there was no Party organisation in Qufu, so the Second Teachers' College branch formed the core of the Party leadership in Qufu County.

In 1928, the Party organisation was destroyed when large-scale combing-out operations were carried out and six members of the Communist Party were arrested. The Shandong Provincial Branch of the Kuomintang was set up in the college and the situation took a rapid turn for the worse. But because the Party had established a firm base among the students, they united and fought back, forcing the Kuomintang to release the arrested students. At this time Song Huanwu, a left-wing member of the Kuomintang and a graduate of Beijing University, took up the post of college dean. He considered himself a student of Lu Xun,[1] whom he held in veneration, and supported the students in their progressive activities. He re-established the disbanded Student Society, organised a student club and a theatre group. Professor Chu Tunan openly gave classes on Marxism-Leninism and dialectical materialism, injecting the student movement with a new lease of life. The call to overthrow the Confucian Curiosity Shop rose to a higher pitch as students printed leaflets condemning the Kong Mansion and raised the slogans 'Down with Madame Tao!', 'Down with the Confucian Curiosity Shop!', 'Down with Local Tyrants and Evil Gentry!' and 'Release the Hundred Households'. The students organised many Temple households and tenants of sacrificial fields, who demonstrated in the street outside our gates, shouted slogans, and covered the high walls of the Kong Mansion with posters. They also chalked slogans all over the trees in the Forest of Confucius.

Some members of the Kong clan, mainly young students, also became involved in the anti-Confucian movement and joined in their demonstrations. Some students named Kong even changed their names to demonstrate their resolution in the cause – one youth

[1] Lu Xun (1881–1936), perhaps the single most important figure in modern Chinese literature, had gone on record in his stories, essays, and lectures as opposing the perpetuation of Confucianism in China because it had been employed to justify a moral tradition that served the interests of the ruling classes.

named Kong Shaohua changed his surname to Gao, though later some of them changed their names back to Kong.

In the days when the tide of anti-Confucianism was sweeping Qufu, the doors of the Kong Mansion were kept tightly closed. Our life went on as before inside the palatial depths of the Inner Apartments. At the time I was only ten or so and couldn't comprehend the seriousness of the situation. Each day I studied and played as usual, only noticing that Madame Tao's face was always drawn in anxiety. She was visited almost every day by the clan chief, Kong Chuanyu and the head of the Confucian Society, Kong Chuanpu. Family elders came and went all day, holding discussions with Madame Tao in the Qianshang Building. We often played there, but were neither interested in nor understood what they were talking about. I remember that at first, Madame Tao was always sending servants outside to erase the chalk slogans from the walls and tear down the brightly coloured posters. Later, the effort was abandoned as hopeless. In fact, we were delighted that Madame Tao was kept so busy, because in this way she had no time to bother about us, and we could play to our hearts' content without the slightest fear of being rebuked for not being 'sedate'.

Later we heard that the students were performing a play called *Confucius Meets Duchess Nanzi*, written by Lin Yutang[1] and published in the progressive magazine *Torrent* (*Benliu*). The students of the Second Teachers' College altered the script, completely changing the image presented of Confucius. We all clamoured to see the play, particularly since we'd heard that there were girl students taking part – a real novelty. In the past all women's roles in drama were played by men, and women never took to the stage. But the moment we mentioned the play, Madame Tao's countenance took on a highly distressed look. Many of the servants had seen the play, so we surreptitiously asked them about it: all they would say was that it portrayed Confucius, and further enquiries only brought a shake of the head and silence. This only added to our curiosity to see our ancestor's image on stage. The excitement caused by the play rose to a higher pitch and we heard that members

---

[1] Lin Yutang (1895–1976), a writer and journalist known in the West for his English-language works like *The Importance of Living* and novels set in China. Before he left China for the USA in 1936 he was a progressive critic.

of other Mansions had all been given tickets, and that it was being performed several times a day to packed houses. Finally one day after the Double Tenth Festival, when the red festival lanterns were still hanging over the gates of every house, we managed to see it.

Madame Tao led the three of us to the platform in the Eastern College where it was possible to see over the wall to the stage in the street opposite. The platform was hung with a curtain so that we couldn't be seen from outside. I recall that I was most deeply impressed by the fright I felt when Confucius appeared on stage – the image was entirely different from his statue in the Hall of Great Achievements. He still wore his ceremonial hat and a gown, but his face was coarse and vulgar and smeared all over with kettle-black. A beautiful woman was sitting in a Buddha niche, bedecked with jade pendants and pearls. Someone told me: 'That's Nanzi!'

Nanzi handed Confucius a piece of green jade, which I could see was a piece of green soap. Zi Lu, Confucius' famous disciple, appeared on stage in a bright red gown and with a red face, also looking quite different from his portrait. I still remember Confucius pointing to heaven and bellowing at Zi Lu: 'If I had wrong ideas, Heaven would detest me.' Below the stage the sound of clapping mingled with shouts of 'Down with the Confucian Curiosity Shop', 'Down with Madame Tao'. I sat at Madame Tao's side and although she remained silent, I could feel her whole body shaking. Turning to look at her I found her face ashen, clouded by an unforgettable expression of gloom.

When the play finished, Madame Tao led us down the earth pile and back to the Inner Apartments without uttering a sound. We had just reached the Qiantang Building when a servant came bringing news: Uncle Kong Lingyu was dead. Since my father's death, Kong Lingyu had handled all Mansion affairs, and during the anti-Confucian movement it was he who had dealt with the disturbances. A short while before, he had been too ill to leave his bed, but still continued to direct Mansion affairs. To Madame Tao, beset with domestic and external problems alike, his death was another severe blow. Hearing the news, she fell paralysed on her bed and remained a hemiplegic until her death.

Kong Lingyu was dead, Madame Tao paralysed and the Second Teachers' College anti-Confucian movement in the ascendant. The head of the Confucian Society Kong Chuanpu and the clan chief

Kong Chuanyu organised members of the Clan Council to petition the Central Education Department, denouncing the Second Teachers' College and the students responsible for the play. It was said that Kong Xiangxi (H. H. Kung) lent his support by speaking on the Mansion's behalf in the central government organs. Chiang Kai-shek personally reprimanded He Siyuan, head of the Shandong Province Education Department and directed him to investigate the allegations.

Later I heard that Chiang Kai-shek hoped to use this case to elbow local powers in Shandong Province out of the way, and place the province under the control of his own clique. He Siyuan saw through this and was unwilling to handle the case. At the same time the anti-Confucian movement found support among members of the central government, and Cai Yuanpei and Jiang Menglin made an unsuccessful attempt to have the sacrificial field system abolished. Unable to convince the central government to act on the Mansion's behalf, Kong Chuanpu made a second report to the county government, and a trial was held to settle the matter. Unexpectedly, the opening session turned out to be a farce: representing the plaintiff were Kong Chuanpu, Kong Chuanyu and a dozen or so septuagenarians, while the defendants sent a dozen ten-year-old school children who all claimed to be actors. Old men were bringing action against small children; it was impossible for the case to proceed. Kong Chuanpu was so furious that he had to be carried out of court. He died shortly afterwards.

The county government dealt with the case by demanding that the heads of the students' families publish an apology to the plaintiff in the local newspaper. Later the college dean, Song Huanwu, was transferred out of the area and two students were expelled.

According to the family elders, the two leading actors – Qiu Senlin, who played Confucius, and Chen Zhensi, who played Nanzi – were in desperate straits at school. The girl, Chen Zhensi, was forced to abandon her studies and joined the revolution. Later she was arrested by the Kuomintang and died a martyr's death at the Rain Flower Terrace in Nanjing.

Several decades later, thinking back on these events, I feel that *Confucius Meets Duchess Nanzi* and the momentous anti-Confucian movement were quite different from a correct evaluation of Confucius. Two thousand years of feudal rule had brought about changes in Confucius' doctrine, altering it as was necessary to maintain the power of the ruling class. Confucius had become a concrete symbol of rule by the feudal ethical code. 'Down with the Confucian Curiosity Shop' was an anti-feudal slogan, but Confucius himself was an eminent thinker, educator and philosopher, whose contributions to Chinese culture cannot be obliterated – over 2,000 years of history have already proven this.

The Yan-Feng War Against Chiang Kai-shek

In February 1929, Madame Tao died, and in April of the next year, the Yan-Feng-Chiang Incident occurred. War came to Qufu.

I was about ten years old at the time and had lived all my life in the Inner Apartments of the Kong Mansion in total ignorance of the outside world. Before the war broke out, I had no idea of the danger that would befall us.

One day, I was playing with my brother in the courtyard of the Qiantang Building when we suddenly heard far off the sound of cannonfire. The booming drew closer and grew more violent. We had no idea what was going on. The old maidservants pulled us inside the building, while outside we heard the cry: 'War! War! They're attacking us!' People started to scurry about piling up tables and chairs and covering them with thick quilts. I was squeezed in under a huge table and my brother was pushed into a triangular niche under the wooden staircase. The table and staircase were piled high with quilts and we were instructed to remain where we were. By this time, fragments of shrapnel were flying through the courtyard and embedding themselves in the walls, which fortunately were too thick for them to pass through. We squatted in our hiding places hearing people commenting that this was a battle between the armies of Yan Xishan and the Kuomintang, but only after the battle was over did we learn the details: Yan's army had been attacking Shandong for over a month, so the Kuomintang Government sent a punitive expedition which engaged Yan's army northeast of Qufu. In the fierce battle that ensued, Chiang Kai-shek's troops proved no match for their opponents, and at dusk they retreated to Qufu to make a stand in the town. Yan's army completely surrounded the town, bombarding it with heavy shell fire.

Yan attacked the town with three divisions, while the Kuomintang troops under a single brigade commander held the town successfully for eleven days. As heavy cannonfire struck Qufu, the townsfolk fled to seek refuge in the Kong Mansion and Temple of Confucius. Even the Inner Apartments were overflowing with refugees. People even slept under Madame Tao's bier where it lay in the Qianshang Building.

Although fewer shells landed in the Mansion and Temple than outside, serious damage was done to fifteen different sections of the Temple buildings. A hole was blown in the northwest corner of the Kui Literature Pavilion and the upper layer of its upturned eaves was damaged. The ceiling of the Hall of Great Achievements was also punctured. Outside the Kong Mansion, the devastation was even worse. The Temple to Yan Hui was hit in over thirty places and buildings in the east, west and north of the town were destroyed. Altogether 3,000 soldiers sheltered were killed or wounded.

One shell landed on the staircase where my brother was hiding, but it rolled down the stairs without exploding. Another shell landed before the statue of Confucius in the Hall of Great Achievements, but also failed to explode. Afterwards the legend grew up that heaven had protected our sagely ancestor and the young sage, but in fact many shells failed to detonate: one passed clean through the Hall of Loyalty and Forbearance without exploding, and another fell harmlessly onto the Red Calyx Hall.

Decheng and I lay besieged for eleven days and nights, eating and sleeping under the staircase and the table, never once permitted to venture out. Rumours ran rife through the town and the populace remained on tenterhooks. People said that after entering the town, the Yan army was planning to violate all unmarried girls, so the maidservants, afraid for my safety, dressed me up as a young married woman, changing my hairstyle from the single plait of a girl to the coiled bun of a married woman. They dressed me in the clothes of a peasant woman and changed Decheng's apparel to coarse peasant clothing.

Life was extremely difficult in those eleven days. The Kong Mansion was overcrowded, the main problem being the lack of water. Ordinarily a cart was sent daily to the south gate of the city to fetch water, but as this became impossible, we had to rely on a bitter well in the Eastern College. Not only was the water bitter, there was simply not enough of it: one well couldn't possibly provide drinking water for thousands of people. People became ill and there were neither doctors nor medicine to treat them. Even food was running out. The defence garrison's ammunition was almost spent, but Yan's divisions were bombarding the town even more heavily than before. The attacking army sent an ultimatum to the town: if the gates were not opened by a given time, poison gas would be released. Heavy artillery was moved into position outside the walls and everyone in the town and the Kong Mansion was consumed with anxiety.

At this critical juncture, Chiang Kai-shek's reinforcements arrived, attacking Yan from the northeast. Yan's troops fled north, suffering heavy casualties.

After the battle, the Kong Mansion circulated a letter of appeal in Decheng's name to powers both Chinese and foreign mentioning various historical precedents of battles near holy areas of shrines. The example was cited of how when battling armies of European powers discovered themselves in the vicinity of Jerusalem, both sides were careful to protect the holy city; but here the Yan army had the audacity to aim their cannons at China's sacred ground, the Kong Mansion and Temple of Confucius. This was an outrage of proportions rarely witnessed in China or in any country.[1] At their request for aid, Chiang Kai-shek and others sent personal telegrams

[1] The exact text of Kong Decheng's original message reads:

'Xuzhou Field Headquarters, Generalissimo Chiang Kai-shek and Eminent Persons in all Fields:

A war has just taken place in the vicinity of the sacred Forest at Qufu. Cannonfire was directed at us, shells fell in the sacred Forest, struck the city walls and shook the Temple of Confucius. Such a dangerous situation left me at a total loss as to what to do. Consider that in past years, when engaged in battle, European armies without exception remained a minimum of ten miles from Jerusalem, a city sacred to the memory of Jesus Christ. Throughout the world, our sage Confucius is recognised as being of quintessential importance to Chinese culture, and Qufu is the location of his sacred Temple and Forest. Our first president, Sun Yat-sen, inherited the ways of the sage and frequently expressed his deep reverence for Confucius in his speeches. Our Generalissimo has also issued an enlightened order to protect the holy sites . . .'

After the war we took medicine for several months to cure a mysterious illness

expressing their condolences. The telegram Chiang Kai-shek sent to Decheng in reply ran as follows:

> July 23, 19th year of the Republic Mr Kong Decheng and the members of the Confucian Society.
>
> The recent damage to the Forest and Temple of Confucius and the injury and death suffered by the people, were caused solely by the traitor from Shanxi besieging and bombarding the town with heavy artillery fire. That a man who claims to revere the sage and observe the rites should wreak this destruction on the holy shrine was totally unexpected and a great source of sorrow and dismay to me. My generals and troops have always considered it their duty to protect the people's lives and property. I have already telegraphed ordering the commander-in-chief of the region to issue orders that officers and men are to safeguard the Temple and Forest at any cost.
>
> Generalissimo Chiang Kai-shek

Qufu Falls into Enemy Hands

After the Japanese invasion in 1937, Decheng left home for Chong-qing, and for eight years Qufu remained in enemy hands. In this period, the economic position of the Kong Mansion changed for the better primarily because Decheng was not at home during the war and only one relative remained to look after the Mansion; few guests came to visit, and entertainment costs were greatly reduced. Secondly, sacrificial ceremonies were carried out with much less grandeur than before. The masters of sacrificial ceremonies thought out various ways to cut expenses which at the same time saved

---

which we were suffering from. What it was I don't know; it was probably caused by extreme terror!

When the battle was over, stories began to circulate through the town that the defeat and flight of Yan's army was not due to the arrival of reinforcements, but to the appearance on the city walls of a huge dark-skinned man sent from heaven to rescue the town. In those times, when science was still a thing of the future, any strange phenomenon, particularly anything that happened at Qufu, was attributed to supernatural causes, often related to the Kong Mansion.

themselves a great deal of trouble. For example, according to the regulations, the Hall of Great Achievement alone had to be supplied with twenty kilos of sacrificial rice-wine in a huge bronze vat, not to mention the secondary halls and side halls. The masters of ceremonies reduced this to a maximum of one and a half to two and a half kilos, making up the difference with water. The sacrificial meat was replaced by vegetables covered with a few meat slices, and sometimes deep-fried cakes were used as a substitute. The numbers of pigs, sheep and oxen used in sacrifices remained unchanged, but much smaller animals were used. Later it became common practice for the two head masters of ceremonies, Ma Zhenhai and Ma Gui, to go to the butchers and just borrow meat. It would be laid out as stipulated in the rituals and returned to the butcher. The two Mas made a profit from this: according to the old rules, all sacrificial officials received a portion of the sacrificial meat after the ceremony. The Ma brothers' method was to deposit the money which was supposed to be used to purchase sacrificial meat in an 'account' at the butcher's, and borrowed meat on this account. When they had accumulated sufficient 'credit', they could easily afford to buy an entire sheep or pig for themselves.

During the Japanese occupation, the Japanese government was eager to win the trust of the people and made efforts to safeguard historical sites like the Kong Mansion and Temple of Confucius, and to show respect for the sage. Japanese army officers often came to the Temple of Confucius to burn incense. After performing a ritual bow, they would make donations which the Temple attendants would record along with the donor's name on a wooden board in front of the altar. The next Japanese officer to come to the Temple would invariably out-give his predecessor. By the end of the month, the board would be covered with names and sums, and each month a new board would be erected. The Kong Mansion used this money to pay many minor daily expenses. It no longer had to borrow money, and even redeemed some of the land it had mortgaged out.

The Japanese army treated the Kong Mansion with respect though they brutally punished people in the Mansion who engaged in anti-Japanese activities.

The first action of the Japanese army after arriving in Qufu was to put up a huge notice on the notice board outside the Second Hall. It read: 'Respect and safeguard the residence of the descendants of the sage. No member of the Japanese forces is permitted to enter.' When the Japanese troops read the notice, many of them bowed to it, then turned and left. They neither entered the Mansion nor destroyed anything. When Decheng left the Mansion, he left a box of biscuits in his bedroom. On his return eight years later he found it untouched.

The Japanese army often appropriated carts and drivers in the street, so a small yellow pennant was fixed to the front of our water cart to indicate its origins. In the same way, the families employed by the Kong Mansion all pasted paper strips over their doors reading: 'Family in the employ of the Mansion of the Sage'.

In the occupied areas, the Japanese troops often broke into people's houses, raping and pillaging. But because the Kong Mansion was relatively safe in this regard, relatives from the Twelve Mansions and the families of Kong Mansion footmen and stewards gradually began to move into the Mansion. In addition, others arranged through friends in the Mansion to be allowed to live there. All these people resided in the Eastern College.

At that time, apart from Kong Xiaguang, who presided over sacrifices and managed the internal and external affairs of the Mansion, there was a man called Kong Lianfang who handled business and relations with the local Japanese government. Kong Lianfang had formerly been an official receptionist inside the Mansion, and held office under the Commander of the 72nd Division, Sun Tongxuan. He wore a long gown and spectacles and had a gentle, refined air. He was highly adept at social intercourse and represented the Kong Mansion at sacrifices held to console the spirits at the soldiers' cemetery, in setting up a preliminary meeting of the New People's Society, in arranging propaganda lectures by the Japanese, in establishing the prefectural office, and in discussions on rebuilding the town wall. The Japanese army frequently held meetings in the Kui Literature Pavilion in the Temple of Confucius, and it was always Kong Lianfang who supervised arranging tables, chairs and tea bowls. But unfortunately he had a poor relationship with his wife. She would often chase him along the street scolding him, and soon he became the laughing stock of Qufu. Later he abandoned his mother, wife and children, eloped with another woman and was never heard of again. After the

Anti-Japanese War, Decheng took over responsibility for supporting this man's old mother.

In the period of occupation, the Japanese ran classes in the Confucian classics and opened a library containing materials relating to Confucian studies. Failing to secure Kong Mansion approval to hold them in the Mansion, they took place in the Changdu Temple.

During this period, the number of security troops guarding the Mansion increased to more than 300, with over half of them stationed inside the compound. But in fact they were security troops in name alone. They had been sent by the Japanese invaders to 'guard' us, but it was only the Japanese army itself which had the power to harass the Mansion.

While Qufu was under Japanese occupation, the Chinese Communist Party carried out a great deal of underground work in the Qufu area. A chief underground leader was one of my 'grandfathers' from the Fifth Mansion, Kong Fanren. Although in terms of generation he was a senior member of the clan, he was actually still a young man. He had joined the Communist underground while a university student in Beijing before the outbreak of the Anti-Japanese War, and after the war began was sent back to Qufu by the Party. As a teacher at the Second Teachers' College, he carried out anti-Japanese propaganda and organisational work, and recruited several new Party members. He organised progressive students, issued anti-Japanese handbills, and held secret meetings to promote anti-Japanese patriotic ideas. Because the members of the Twelve Mansions were living in the Eastern College at the time, he was able to do a lot of work amongst his young relatives. They and other family members sympathetic to the anti-Japanese cause would often dress up as peasants in straw hats and coarse blue and white striped jackets and trousers and carry out propaganda work in the countryside. Some of the family realised what was happening, but no one said anything. They just commented behind their backs: 'These youngsters aren't content to enjoy their good fortune. They have to go out of their way to make things difficult for themselves!'

Later Kong Fanren assigned a student named Yan to work on anti-Japanese propaganda, intending to help him to join the Party. Yan appeared to be an enthusiastic activist, but was actually an informer. The situation had become very tense and Kong Fanren decided to flee by night, but that same day five truckloads of Japanese soldiers surrounded the Second Teachers' College and seized seven people whom Yan had betrayed. The Japanese brought Kong Fanren back to the Mansion and conducted a search. His clothes were torn to shreds and his arms were bound, yet when his Japanese captors relaxed their vigilance for a moment, he tried to break away and commit suicide by jumping into a well. But the guards recaptured him before he'd gone more than a few paces, beat him viciously with the butts of their guns and kicked him with their hobnailed boots until his face was streaming with blood. That same day he was sent under escort to the headquarters of the Japanese military police in Yanzhou and tortured in an attempt to force him to confess, but he never said a word. Later he was taken to Jinan where he was eventually executed. Another of my distant relatives was also jailed in the military police headquarters at Jinan at the time. After his release he told us that he had seen Kong Fanren on trial in court. He had been beaten almost beyond recognition, yet still refused to answer any questions. There was a small door in the courtroom through which condemned criminals were dragged. He saw Kong Fanren walk proudly through it, head held high.

Kong Fanren was 41 years old when he died. He left an old mother and a wife and three children, the eldest seven, the youngest just a few months old.

Only after the founding of the People's Republic was Yan brought to justice. The People's Government condemned him to death and the notice of his execution was posted on the gate of the Drum Tower.

6

My Younger Brother Kong Decheng

Sibling Affection

From the whisperings of our maidservants and family members, we three children knew from an early age how kind our natural mother, Concubine Wang, had been. And we knew as well how she had been poisoned by Madame Tao. Although we lived with Madame Tao, there was no affection between us, and all aspects of our relationship ran in strict accordance with the Confucian ethical code and clan rules. Our father died early, and with no other close relations, we developed an unusual affection for each other. We never quarrelled among ourselves or threw tantrums. I remember how we would sweep our mother's grave each year. We three small children would go to the vast Forest, and after kowtowing before her grave, sat in silence, lost in thought. At such times I felt especially close to my brother and sister, as if they were the only relations I had in the whole world.

My elder sister, Kong Deqi, married the youngest son of Feng Shu, a noted Beijing calligrapher and third-place winner in the Qing imperial examinations. After the founding of the Republic, his family opened the Beijing Electric Lamp Company which he personally managed. Mrs Feng came to Qufu many times. She was a kind, motherly woman and extremely fond of me.

At first she wanted me to marry her son, but the difference in our ages was too great, so she arranged the marriage with my elder sister instead, making me her goddaughter on the wedding day. She sent me silver bowls and chopsticks as gifts.

Deqi was seventeen when she married. Mrs Feng and the Fourth Miss Feng came personally to Qufu to receive her and stayed at the Eastern Fifth Mansion. Fourth Miss Feng got on very well with Deqi and was a great comfort to her in the desolation of her married life.

Two servants, the manservant Wu Jianwen and a maidservant Sister Xi, followed Deqi to Beijing on her marriage, but not long afterwards Sister Xi was sent back again to save the cost of her wages.

After my elder sister's marriage, only my younger brother and I remained in the Kong Mansion. As we grew older, we came to understand more deeply the preciousness of our affection. When I retired for the night, I would stare at my sister's empty bed and feel sad. Studying in the classroom during the day seemed much more lonely without her, so Decheng and I clung even more closely to one another, and rarely sought out other playmates. Decheng was called more and more frequently to meet guests, at which times I would wait all alone for him to come back. We didn't play 'house' or ride hobbyhorses any more, but preferred to stroll in the Rear Flower Garden or in a vegetable garden after finishing our classes. The vegetable garden was separated from the Mansion by a small lane. We would go out of the corner gate by the kitchen, walk around the Yiguan Hall and out of the back gate, without a single servant in attendance. At that time I was mentioned almost every day in Decheng's diary. A short extract of several consecutive entries reads as follows:

March 5: After lunch, Second Sister and I visited the Eastern and Western Fifth Mansions, and the Yiguan Hall in the north section of the Mansion to pay our New Year respects. Returned home at 5:00.

March 7: After finishing classes at 4:00, Second Sister and I went for a stroll in the vegetable garden.

March 8: Second Sister and I read in the study and told each other stories.

March 9: Second Sister and I went to the Forest of Confucius to sacrifice.

March 11: Played ball with Second Sister for two hours, then wrote six paired couplets.

March 12: Finished school at 5:00, then played in the Rear Flower Garden with Second Sister.

March 13: Wrote antithetical couplets at home as the mood took us. At 4:00, strolled in the Rear Flower Garden and at 5:00 returned home.

March 15: Teacher went out, so Second Sister and I talked and told each other stories. At 11:00, ordered the florist to arrange flowers on the long desk. There were narcissi at the front, pink plums at the back, a bowl of fish to the left and a dish of fruit to the right. In addition, four bowls of fresh flowers were placed round a dish of melons. The sight was most impressive.

After her marriage, my elder sister visited us often, accompanied only by her servant Wu Jianwen. From Beijing, she brought small ornaments for our childhood playmates, Zhu Erni and Liu Sanyuan's wife and children; and occasionally she brought us some 'foreign' goods. These were, in fact, nothing more than ordinary household articles, but because life in the Kong Mansion was run entirely according to ancient customs, we found them particularly novel. For example, when Deqi brought a thermos flask, the entire Mansion population crowded round to look at it. Although it was the 1930s, we had never seen a thermos flask before and couldn't understand how it could keep water hot without a fire. The five or six hundred people at the Kong Mansion shared this one thermos flask, so it was treated like a precious treasure.

Deqi also brought us a rubber hot-water bottle – another great novelty. My little brother gave it to Liu Sanyuan as a gift, but when he took it home, Liu's father thought his son had brought home some rare and precious object and insisted that he return it. Had he been given a gold ring or several bags of grain, he would have accepted it readily, but the hot-water bottle struck him as too strange.

One year my sister came back to stay with us for a few days. Old Mrs Feng had died recently and Deqi was wearing mourning clothes – a grey *cheongsam*, white earrings and black leather shoes. She was very melancholy and scarcely spoke. The graceful, carefree manner of her girlhood days had disappeared and when I asked her about her life in Beijing, she refused to answer. But in our hearts we recalled the old saying: 'If you marry a rooster, you must follow a rooster; if you marry a dog, you must follow a dog.' For better or for worse, one had to resign oneself to one's fate. Before Deqi left, we were photographed together on the lawn in the Rear Flower Garden. I have kept the photograph right up to the present day. It was the last photograph of the two of us ever taken.

Only afterwards did I learn that my sister's husband led a life of drunken debauchery. He was constantly asking her for money. Once he bought an automobile which he filled with his girlfriends and personally drove around the town. But because he was not a practised driver, he crashed into a utility pole and lost all his teeth. This we learned secretly from Wu Jianwen on one of his visits to the Kong Mansion. To support her husband's dissipation, Deqi took gold from the Mansion back to Beijing whenever she came to visit us, but because she was afraid of being laughed at, she gave it to Wu Jianwen to carry. In order not to upset her, we avoided bringing up the subject of her husband, or handing her gold, silver or ornaments directly. All we could do was to pretend not to notice her when she fetched these things herself. All of this made me very upset, and my heart ached for her. After my own marriage, I understood her suffering more deeply, for my own situation proved to be identical to hers.

I was engaged at the age of thirteen. I remember I was playing in the garden that afternoon when a maidservant told me that Madame Tao wanted to see me. When I walked into the room, Madame Tao smiled and handed me a small photograph of a young schoolboy. Madame Tao said: 'I've found you some in-law.' I threw down the photograph and ran into the inner room, jumped into bed and let down the curtains. I was so shy and frightened that I didn't come out for a long time. From then on I was considered engaged.

My husband was Ke Changfen, the youngest son of Ke Shaomin, a famous Qing dynasty historian and head of the Institute of Qing Dynastic History. He was a scholar of the Imperial Academy, had tutored Puyi, and after Puyi ascended the throne as the last Qing emperor, was employed at the Yuqing Palace. Ke Shaomin was the sworn brother of Xu Shichang, who thought highly of his talents. When Xu held office as President of the Republic, he gave orders that a *New History of the Yuan Dynasty* as revised by Ke Shaomin become the twenty-fifth official Chinese dynastic history. Xu Shichang also married one of his granddaughters to one of Ke's grandsons. Ke Shaomin's wife was Wu Zhifang, the daughter of a famous Qing prose writer, Wu Rulun, and herself an accomplished poet. Her elder sister, Wu Zhiying, was also a talented scholar and had been a friend of the Qing revolutionary heroine Qiu Jin. When Qiu Jin was executed, it was Wu Zhiying who took care of Qiu's remains.

Ke Shaomin had three sons; the two eldest, Ke Changsi and Ke Changji, were both scholars researching oracle-bone characters, but the third son, Changfen, had been spoiled since birth and was a good-for-nothing.

Both Deqi and my own marriages were arranged by Madame Tao in Beijing. Madame Tao claimed this was because it was difficult to find an appropriate match anywhere else, but I suspect other reasons were involved. In our childhood, Madame Tao had taken us to Beijing to her family home and her relatives frequently visited the Kong Mansion, helping her to consolidate her power. Madame Tao hoped to marry us into Beijing families close to her own as a way of maintaining her family's control over the Kong Mansion.

I was married the year my younger brother turned fifteen. Three days before my wedding, he gave me a wedding gift – several hundred boxes containing my dowry, the first containing a large *ruyi*, a good luck charm supposed to bring its owner all that he or she wished for.

The Kong Mansion had two priceless treasures handed down from the ancestors – two fine wooden *ruyi* the size of a writing desk carved with a hundred young children bearing different expressions and in different postures. In the centre was the figure of an old man representing King Wen of the Zhou dynasty, the father of the hundred sons. These were given to Deqi and me as part of our dowries.

Wooden *ruyi* of this quality was given only to important guests of the Kong Mansion. According to legend, after the death of Confucius, his favourite disciple Zi Gong stood watch over his grave for six years. As he finally prepared to leave the graveside, he stuck his mourning staff of pistachio wood into the ground where it was watered by his falling tears. There it took root and grew into a huge tree. Later, the descendants of Confucius presented a small *ruyi* of pistachio wood to their most distinguished guests, while ordinary guests received one of gold or jade. Each of us also received a pair of huge gold bells inlaid with diamonds and pearls belonging to the Mansion. Actually, many items in our dowries were identical; sadly enough, our fates were identical too.

Decheng escorted me to my wedding held in the Sun Family Mansion in Qufu. My father-in-law, Ke Shaomin, was seriously ill, so Ke Changsi, my husband's eldest brother, accompanied the groom from Beijing. On my wedding day, I awoke very early.

Mother Wang dressed my hair for me, after which I ate two boiled eggs, changed into my wedding clothes and went to wait in the central room of the Qiantang Building for the bridal sedan chair to fetch me. All the footmen and maidservants were wearing new short blue cotton gowns. I was wearing the traditional bridal phoenix coronet and red cape and was carried out in a gold-roofed bridal sedan chair with eight bearers. A memorial arch of red cloth had been erected at the Main Gate of the Mansion and coloured marquees were placed in the courtyard. Crowds of sightseers gathered outside the Mansion gates. The sound of music and firecrackers was endless, lulling me into a daze from which I could see and hear nothing clearly. It was one of the hottest days of summer and I was wearing a phoenix coronet, a mass of pearls and jade, the red cape and a long, heavy skirt. The perspiration pouring off me stained my underwear with red dye, but I was unaware of this at the time.

The next morning, Decheng came to visit me at the Sun Mansion and in the afternoon I returned home for a ritual visit. A banquet was held in the open-air pavilion in the Rear Flower Garden. I had originally intended to remain at Qufu for a few days, but three days after the wedding an urgent telegram arrived from Beijing to say that Ke Shaomin was critically ill, so I made preparations to leave. When I stepped into the carriage, I was wearing a pink *cheongsam* embroidered with a large phoenix. Wiping away my tears, I bade a last farewell to all my relatives, my home and my beloved brother, and set out for the capital.

Several days before my marriage, my brother completely lost his appetite. I still remember what he said to me when I left: 'With you and Deqi gone, I'll be the only one in the Mansion.' His face was clouded with sadness, without a trace of childishness in his expression.

The day after I left Qufu, Decheng became ill. Liu Mengying was not in Qufu at the time, so a Doctor Qiao treated him. Whether because Qiao was not a skilled doctor, or for some other reason, Decheng's condition did not improve for many days. Decheng's teacher lived with him in the school courtyard while he was ill, and when he began to recover prohibited him from going to the Rear Flower Garden or the Inner Apartments for fear of reviving painful memories. He often took Decheng to watch opera at the Temple of the Three Emperors, or to eat at the Yanbin Restaurant. On the anniversary of Third Grandfather's birthday, he invited Decheng to a feast to enliven his spirits. My little brother was very grateful for his teacher's concern, but nothing seemed to be able to cheer him up. After my marriage he picked a new name for himself – Jieyu (solitary) – which aptly revealed his state of mind. He used this name frequently to sign his many poems; although these poems were not outstanding literary works, they moved me greatly. In the desolation of my unhappy marriage, I missed my family deeply, and whenever I read my brother's verses, silent tears would pour down my cheeks. Decades later I still recall a few of them:

Yearning for Second Sister
In the dusk I gaze northwards along distant paths;
When kindred are apart, the tears will never dry.
The distant mountains are shrouded in mist;
Alone I hear the wild swan's mournful cry.

Night Rain
As the third watch sounds, the rain falls;
And my thoughts turn to sisters far away.
Beyond gauze curtains, cold as ice,
Raindrops splash down from the silent leaves.

After my marriage, I returned to the Kong Mansion often, sometimes with my sister and sometimes alone. Every time I went back, my brother went mad with delight; he would take a holiday from school and spend the day accompanying me around.

At this time my brother devoted all his energy to his studies. If guests arrived, he would return to his study the moment they had left without any prompting from his teacher. He gradually cast off his childish ways and his thinking began to mature. Besides attending his formal classes he loved to study the rites of Dong Zhongshu.

My sister and I both lived in the western part of Beijing. She lived in Mutton Alley and I lived on nearby Taipusi Street. We visited each other frequently and Deqi seemed much happier. But when our thoughts turned to our marital relationships, we would sit together in silence, reluctant – due to our traditional ethical upbringing – to speak a word against our husbands. Not long after my marriage, my husband was posted to Tianjin and I was obliged to go along. So Deqi and I were separated once again.

One day while I was living in Tianjin, an urgent telegram arrived from Fourth Miss Feng informing me that my sister was critically ill. I returned to Beijing straight away to find Deqi already unconscious. The famous Beijing doctor, Kong Bohua, had just finished examining her, but he said very little; after writing out a prescription, he left. I fed her the medicine spoonful by spoonful, but Deqi could hardly swallow it. When she regained consciousness momentarily she had to summon all of her strength just to whisper: 'Don't give me any more.' Her lips trembled as if she were trying to speak, but no sounds came out. She looked at me with infinite sadness, cold tears filling her eyes. Minutes later she was dead.

Shortly after my sister stopped breathing, her lips and fingernails turned black, a sign that she had taken poison. This was in the period of the Anti-Japanese War, and with Decheng far away in Chongqing, the family at the Kong Mansion sent a relative to handle legal matters in his place. As there was a strong suspicion that Deqi had committed suicide, the family resolved to take the Feng family to court, and gave money to the relative who was to act as plaintiff to cover costs. The Feng family feared their reputation would be badly damaged if news of the affair leaked out, so they bribed the plaintiff with 500 silver dollars. As a result, the case never went to court, and the 'plaintiff' absconded with both the court fees and the 500 dollars. Only later did we learn that he went to Qingdao to enjoy the good life. After the Anti-Japanese War, Decheng went to sacrifice at the Fayuan Temple where my sister's coffin was resting. He remained before the coffin for many hours, stricken with grief.

A year after Deqi died, my husband, my child and I moved back to our old residence on Taipusi Street in Beijing.

The Ke family residence was a huge mansion. Its eastern courtyard and surrounding buildings had been forcibly occupied by a high-ranking Japanese military police officer, and part of the rear section was rented out to the acting Police Commissioner. This left us with forty or fifty rooms to ourselves. My two brothers-in-law lived independently away from home; my two sisters-in-law had married and moved away; and my father-in-law had died, so the mansion was very quiet.

My husband came home rarely, but when he did it was generally to demand money and jewellery from me. At the Kong Mansion, I never saw anyone fly into rages as he did, and thus I had no idea how to handle him. Only Mother Wang dared argue with him, but she finally had to return to Qufu. Eventually my entire dowry including jewellery, money, stone rubbings, calligraphy and paintings all passed into his hands.

Deqi was dead. Decheng was far away in Chongqing. Without close relatives at the Kong Mansion, there was no reason for me to go back. So I remained alone in Beijing with my two children.

Behind my bedroom and connected to it by a small door, was the Knotweed Garden, a flower garden that took its name from the plant that grew there. I spent hours there each day, strolling or just sitting idly, very much missing my home-town and my brother and sister. There is a saying, 'At festival time, the absence of loved ones is felt more deeply.' Each year at the Mid-Autumn Festival, my thoughts would turn to the two huge pomegranate trees in the Qianshang Building Courtyard of the Kong Mansion Inner Apartments – my brother and I loved to pick the pomegranates at this time of year – so I had a pomegranate tree planted on either side of our door in the garden. I remembered how we three children loved to play under the wintersweet tree by the schoolroom, and had one planted in the garden as well. I also installed two huge vats of lotus flowers to remind me of the lotuses in the Rear Flower Garden. Here I would relate stories of the Kong Mansion and my childhood to my daughter.

Adjacent to the Ke Mansion was the Kong Mansion's Beijing residence, the Sage Duke Mansion. Built in the late-Ming to early-Qing period, although smaller than the Kong Mansion, it was still quite large. My father lived there on his trips to Beijing and it was there he died on his last visit to the capital.

With the decline of the Kong Mansion, the Sage Duke Mansion in Taipusi Street also fell into disrepair. The paint began to peel, grass sprouted on the roofs and people from outside the Kong clan began to move in. Most of them lived in the two front courtyards where friends and relatives of family members were permitted. The inner courtyards and central residence still remained the preserve of the Kong family.

Perhaps because they were neighbours, the Kong and Ke families maintained very close relations. My father and father-in-law were intimate friends for many years, and met frequently at the Imperial Palace. Father personally asked Ke Shaomin to inscribe the memorial tablet to be placed in his tomb, and when father was buried along with Madame Tao and my mother, this promise was kept.

There was a distant uncle of mine living in the Sage Duke Mansion who was the blood brother of Ke Changsi. He had acted as matchmaker for both my sister and me, but since both our marriages had turned sour, we had very little to do with him.

In the innermost courtyard of the Sage Duke Mansion lived an old lady, five generations my senior, a noble and respected member of the family with whom I had a very close friendship. It was she who arranged Decheng's marriage to Sun Qifang, one of her fourth-generation nieces.

Members of the family from the Twelve Mansions later moved to the Sage Duke Mansion in Beijing. My Eleventh Aunt, who had been a good friend at the Kong Mansion, visited me often after moving to Beijing. But she proved just as luckless in the end as my sister and I, committing suicide by swallowing opium.

Those were sad times. The women of large clans were all too often forced to play central roles in some tragedy or another. I remember one of my distant relations in the Sage Duke Mansion was a seventy-year-old man who had a very young and beautiful concubine who by the time I moved to Beijing had gone mad. She sat alone all day outside the front gate of the Sage Duke Mansion, alternately laughing and crying. I never learned what drove her mad, but it's easy enough to guess.

A Grand Wedding Ceremony

Kong Decheng Announces
that he and Miss Sun Qifang will hold their
marriage ceremony and wedding feast at
noon on the sixteenth day of the twelfth month.
The pleasure of your company is requested.

Kong Decheng

(The ceremony will be held in the Mansion of the State Master of Sacrifices to Confucius.)

This was the invitation sent out to announce Decheng's wedding. At the time, many newspapers carried reports of his nuptials along with photographs of the ceremony.

Decheng's bride was Sun Qifang of Shouzhou in Anhui Province. She was the granddaughter of Sun Jianai, who had won first place in the imperial examinations and served as Minister of Rites during the Qing dynasty. Sun had also been the chief imperial examiner and held office at the Yuqing Palace as imperial tutor. The Sun family had been scholars for generations. Sun Qifang was a highly cultured young woman. She was eighteen when she married, a year older than Decheng.

The Kong and Sun families held long discussions on the wedding arrangements, and finally decided to hold a wedding which combined the old and new. The bride wore a modern-day white gauze gown and high-heeled shoes specially made in Beijing, but Decheng wore a traditional long gown and mandarin jacket of silk woven with large circular patterns. It was an old-fashioned ceremony performed with the couple kneeling. Large-scale construction was carried out in the Mansion before the wedding, and every wall from the Main Gate to the rear of the Inner Apartments was freshly whitewashed. Other changes were made as well. In the past, two door gods had always been painted on the Main Gate, but for this occasion they were done away with and the gate painted a plain red. Gold dragons on a blue background that had once decorated the roofs were replaced by cloud designs. A stage with seats for the audience on either side was put up outside the Main Gate along with a scarlet decorative archway and red palace lanterns. A pinewood pole was erected in the gateway ready to be hung with strings of firecrackers. The newlyweds were going to live at the Houtang Building in the Inner Apartments, and thus the path between it and the main gate was decorated with coloured marquees supplied by the Kong Mansion's own tentmakers. They were beautiful: the four sides were decorated with coloured glass pictures of five little boys (the 'Five Happinesses') bearing the written character 'longevity', and the roofs were woven of red and green cloth strips. Inside were hung traditional silk congratulatory messages in gold appliqué sent by friends, relatives and officials. These messages alone took twenty factory workers an entire day to hang. Every gateway throughout the Mansion was decorated with coloured lights and palace lanterns. Some lanterns had small bells attached, while others had tassels and fringes. On the day of the wedding, security guards were posted at each gate.

Before the wedding, the rooms in the Eastern College were rearranged to accommodate guests, and a large group of people set to work sewing mattresses and quilts for the visitors. Each of the several hundred servants in the Mansion was given a length of cloth to make themselves a set of new clothes.

The last parcels of the extensive dowry sent from Beijing by the Sun family only arrived one day before the wedding. Originally, the bride's family planned to send a complete set of Western-style furniture, but the Kong Mansion convinced them to revise this plan due to the difficulties of transporting such a large gift. After being unloaded at Yao Village, the dowry was carried to Qufu by bearers wearing red silk cloaks, who were followed by a complete Chinese orchestra. The gold clocks, jewellery, ornaments, bottles, mirrors, cosmetics, brocades, pearls and precious stones overflowed from the courtyard, and many items had to be stored in the newlyweds' quarters, the Houtang Building. There were heaps of clothing and bedding to be stored away as well.

Three days before the wedding, Sun Qifang arrived at Qufu accompanied by her mother and younger sister. They stayed at the Eastern Fifth Mansion in the Shunxian (Abide by Ancestral Ways) Hall.

Deqi was still alive at the time, and we returned to Qufu together with my son Ke Jian, my daughter Ke Lan, my husband Ke Changfen, Deqi's son Zhongshou, her daughter Xiaokang, and assorted servants. We were met at the Yanzhou railway station by the Mansion car (which had already replaced the Mansion horse carriage to become the first motor vehicle in Qufu) and stayed at our old residence, the Qiantang Building.

At the wedding I escorted Decheng to the Eastern Fifth Mansion to receive the bride. The procession was very long: those in front were already inside the Kong Mansion before those in the rear had even left the Shunxian Hall. It was also a synthesis of old and new. In accordance with tradition, five complete operatic orchestras led the procession, while the official insignia – fans, parasols, golden melons, hatchets, and 'heaven facing stools' brought up the rear. Colourfully dressed children walked before the bridal sedan chair carrying two pairs of auspicious white lambs and two huge decorated jugs of wine. A pair of children carried 'sons and grandsons' buckets filled with silver dollars. There was also a child carrying a mirror and one carrying a chafing dish. Each child was given two silver dollars upon arrival at the Kong Mansion.

Decheng received his bride in a green sedan chair, and I rode in the car. One of our elderly women relatives rode in the gold-roofed bridal sedan chair with eight bearers (anyone under the rank of a duke used a silver-roofed chair) to act as 'bride receiving matron'. When we came to the Eastern Fifth Mansion where the bride was staying, Decheng went through the ancient ritual of bending a bow and shooting an arrow, after which the bride was escorted from her room into the bridal sedan chair. She was brought to the main gate of the Eastern Fifth Mansion and then got into the festooned motor car with me. At the gate of the Kong Mansion, she once again changed to the bridal sedan chair and was carried through the Ceremonial Gate to Qianshang Building where the ceremony was to be held. The Qianshang Building Courtyard was laid out with twenty long tables covered with felt tablecloths embroidered around the edges and set with plates full of dragon and phoenix biscuits, 'happiness' salt, dates, chestnuts, lotus seeds, peanuts, pine nuts and longans (to symbolise the early birth of sons and daughters), as well as branches of pine and cypress (symbolising eternal youth), sacrificial offerings and incense burners. The bride dismounted from the sedan chair, stood facing towards the east, and welcomed the God of Good Luck. The moment the bridal sedan chair entered the gate a crowd of reporters in Western suits surged forward to meet it with a flurry of flashbulbs. The bride and I were in long white gowns and high-heeled shoes made to order in Wangfujing Street in Beijing, but since Decheng was to wear a traditional gown and mandarin jacket rather than a formal Western suit, when we had our gowns made, we only ordered outfits for the bride and bridesmaid and nothing for the groom or the best man. The staff of the tailor's shop were completely mystified.

The bride knelt beside Decheng and kowtowed four times in obeisance to heaven and earth. She was then escorted to the Houtang Building to change her outfit. She put on a red velvet *cheongsam* and red satin shoes, twisted her hair up in a bun, and sat down cross-legged under the canopy of the bridal bed in the newlyweds' apartments for several hours until the ceremonies outside were over. Only then did the bridegroom come and drink the nuptial cup with her.

That day three operas were staged at the Mansion: a Shandong clapper ballad was performed in the street outside the Main Gate; a Kunqu Opera[1] was performed in the Third Hall; and a Beijing Opera was performed in the Qianshang Building. Famous performers were engaged from Jinan, Beijing and Tianjin. Programmes were printed for the performances at the Third Hall and the Qianshang Building and were handed out to guests as they arrived, but it rained that day and the large crowd assembled at the Third Hall couldn't fit inside the building, so the performance was moved to the larger Second Hall. Quite a few prominent members of the Kuomintang attended the wedding, and Chiang Kai-shek himself had accepted an invitation. But on December 12th, four days before the wedding, the Xi'an Incident[2] occurred, and Chiang was taken into custody by his generals Zhang Xueliang and Yang Hucheng. We heard nothing about the incident, and received no notice from Chiang Kai-shek saying he could not attend, so the ceremony was delayed until about two o'clock for him. Only when Sun Tongxuan, Commander of the Kuomintang 72nd Division at Yanzhou arrived and told us not to wait for the Generalissimo did the ceremony begin. Chiang's satin congratulatory banner was hung in the centre of the Qianshang Building along with cloud-patterned brocade banners from the central organs of the Kuomintang; the Nationalist Party sent a silver ornamental cooking-pot, while Kong Xiangxi sent another silver ornamental cooking-pot, scrolls gilded with gold, rolls of cloth, and 1,000 dollars. Gifts also arrived from the Japanese Ambassador to China, Shigeru Kawagoe, the Military Attaché of the Japanese Army, Yoshio Ishino, and several other officials.

The tenants of the Kong Mansion also came to offer congratu-

---

[1] Kunqu is a southern form of local opera, see Beijing opera, p. 57.

[2] After the Japanese invasion, many patriots were concerned that Chiang was more interested in persecuting Communists than resisting the Japanese. Zhang Xueliang, who had been driven out of his warlord base in the north east by the Japanese in 1931 and then joined forces with Chiang, kidnapped his superior in an attempt to force him to resist Japan. Ironically, for Chiang was devoting his attention to the persecution of the Communists, he was freed by the intercession of Zhou Enlai.

lations and gifts. They were received under a huge coloured marquee and catered to by the outer kitchen. There were a hundred tables set, with a 'banquet master' responsible for each ten tables. The guests ate whenever they came and the well-wishers arrived in an endless stream. The banquet began in the morning and was still going on at midnight.

The banquet for performers and Mansion employees was handled by the central kitchen, while important guests and relatives were catered to by the inner kitchen. The kitchens only cooked dishes, while the General Affairs Section supplied steamed bread and wine. The inner kitchen feast was held in several rooms of the Inner Apartments – the Hall of Loyalty and Forbearance, the Red Calyx Pavilion, the Flowery Pavilion, the Qiantang Building, etc. – with fifteen tables set in each location. The feast consisted of the standard 'Three Great Items' and 'Nine Great Items'.

The next morning, the new bride paid her respects to my aunt, my sister and myself, as well as to several senior members of the family. A maidservant followed her with a trayful of bowls of sweet longan soup. After the bride and groom kowtowed to the elders, the bride offered them dishes of soup. The elders presented her with 'meeting' gifts – generally simple items like a piece of fabric. These gifts were laid in an exquisite rectangular box covered with a red silk cloth fringed with tassels.

In the early days of their married life, the newlyweds often went on pleasure outings together. At that time, the Kong Mansion had a tiny German car that frequently broke down. The roads around Qufu were very rough and Decheng and Qifang were often forced to get out and push when the car broke down. The couple rarely took any servants along when they went out, and when Qifang went shopping, she would carry her purchases home herself.

They lived in the Houtang Building which was decorated in a combination of Chinese and Western styles. They had Western sofas and old-style wooden tables and chairs. A painting of plum blossoms by the famous Beijing Opera singer Mei Lanfang[1] hung on

---

[1] Mei Lanfang (1894–1961) was one of the greatest Beijing opera performers of the female role. Born into a family of female role players, trained in the traditional style, he brought the opera to the outside world, touring Japan, USSR and America in the 1930s. He was also responsible for modernising some of the plots of operas and for maintaining the popularity of the opera after 1949.

the wall, and a copy of the *Classic of Filial Piety* lay on a table. They continued to live there until they moved to Chongqing on the eve of the Japanese invasion.

State Master of Sacrifices

As a child, my younger brother often accompanied Madame Tao when she received reports on Mansion affairs. Sitting at a long desk in the Qianshang Building, she listened to officials and accountants making their various reports and examined all kinds of official documents. The year Decheng turned nine, Madame Tao became a hemiplegic, so he took over sole nominal responsibility for this work. He didn't preside over the long desk but while we were playing together, Third Grandfather, Kong Yinqiu, would come and confer with him. Kong Yinqiu was renowned for his sincere honesty and loyalty to the clan. After my uncle died, he was asked to take charge of the external affairs of the Mansion. He had great reverence for my younger brother and would come every day to explain Mansion affairs to him and seek his opinions. Decheng often said to him: 'Third Grandfather, I'm very young and don't understand these things. You do as you see fit.' But regardless of the matter at hand, Kong Yinqiu always obtained Decheng's approval for the solution he had put forward. When Decheng and I were playing hide-and-seek in the caves in the Rear Flower Garden or 'performing' operas for each other, Kong Yinqiu would often appear with a document drafted by the Head Secretary of the Mansion, Chen Yunlang. Decheng would take a writing brush and scrawl a word of approval in cursive script, whereupon we would resume our games.

In the winter of 1924, the Kong Mansion enlarged the Four Clans Teachers' College into the Queli Manifest Virtue Middle School. Since those were deemed times when 'virtue was obscured' and the 'classics had been abandoned', the school was established with a mission to 'make virtue manifest'. The school opened formally in the spring of the following year, and Decheng, then five, was appointed headmaster. Later, he supplemented his lessons at the family school with daily English lessons there, so he was simultaneously both headmaster and student.

Guests from China and abroad frequently visited the Mansion and on these occasions, my brother would be taken to meet them. For this he had to learn a set of elaborate formalities. Important guests were entertained with a *gaobai* feast of over 130 dishes, but according to etiquette, Decheng could only eat sparingly. He would often start complaining of hunger the moment the guests had left and would have to eat another meal.

Important political and military figures, including Chiang Kai-shek, visited the Mansion on a private informal basis, while others like Kong Xiangxi paid imposing formal visits. In each case, the Kong Mansion would be roused to a fever of activity making preparations. Sun Ke, the son of Sun Yat-sen, and the 'Christian General' Feng Yuxiang came to visit and wrote several commemorative poems. Han Fuju, Chairman of the Shandong Provincial Government, a coarse, vulgar man, was a frequent guest. Dai Chuanxian, one of the top administrative heads of the Kuomintang, was a bit more refined, and generous with his praise of Decheng. He presented him with a copy of the *Classic of Filial Piety* hand-copied by his mother.

Guests often brought gifts with them and the Kong Mansion would present gifts in return – usually rubbings from ancient stone carvings dating as far back as the Han dynasty (206 BC–AD 220). Because they were rare, many high-ranking Kuomintang officials who understood nothing of their cultural value demanded them merely for the sake of their monetary worth. Not only was the Kong Mansion unable to keep up with the demand, but the large numbers of rubbings being made were damaging the ancient stone tablets. We couldn't afford to offend the Kuomintang, so another solution to the problem had to be found. Only when some of the most valuable stone tablets were covered with strips of yellow paper to protect them from avaricious eyes did things take a turn for the better.

Mass organisations also came to visit: a Beijing University tour group and a Jinan tour group both came to meet the 'young sage'. My younger brother received them in one of the outer guest halls and was photographed with them.

Sometimes Decheng would make formal visits outside the Mansion: when Han Fuju's son got married, he went to Jinan to offer his congratulations. But he didn't always attend in person:

when the famous capitalist Hardoon died in Shanghai, he simply sent a eulogy by mail.

We also entertained many foreign guests. Before they arrived, the Kuomintang or Kong Xiangxi would inform us and we would prepare a magnificent reception and meet them at Yanzhou. When the guests left, Decheng returned to the library and resumed his studies, or went for a stroll with me.

In 1935, Chiang Kai-shek decided to change Decheng's title from the Yansheng Duke to 'State Master of Sacrifices to the Exalted Sage and First Teacher' and granted him the stipend of a special-status official. In June of the same year, Decheng, Yan Shiyong, Meng Qingtang and Zeng Fanshan (the direct descendants of Yan Hui, Mencius and Zengzi) went to Jinan to meet the top provincial officials and then took the train to Nanjing. On July 8th at a ceremony conducted by Chen Lifu, one of the top leaders of the Kuomintang, Decheng swore an oath to Dai Chuanxian and formally assumed office. Afterwards, he detoured to Shanghai to pay his respects to Kong Xiangxi and was entertained with a lavish banquet. This was the first time he had travelled such a long distance from home, and as usual he was accompanied by Chen Jingrong and Wu Jianzhang. While in Shanghai, Decheng personally chose several pieces of fabric and sent them to me in Beijing.

The Shanghai Confucian Society held an enthusiastic welcome ceremony for Decheng, who made a speech of thanks. After returning to Qufu, he placed his new seal of office in the Great Hall and called in a goldsmith from Jinan to prepare it for use. It was a square seal engraved with the words: 'For a civil official, justice and impartiality should be the most ennobling goals.' As the goldsmith put the finishing touches on the seal, coloured buntings fluttered in the gateways and strings of firecrackers were set off in a celebration as grand as an elaborate wedding.

Decheng's appointment to the post of State Master of Sacrifices brought about some changes in the staff of the Mansion. In addition to the original servants of the Forest and Temple of Confucius, a new class of receptionists was added who wore the uniforms of personal attendants. Since classical music and dance were becoming lost arts, a Classical Music Institute was established in the Eastern College. Eighty students were enrolled and Decheng himself acted as dean with administration heads, professors and an entire staff underneath his direction.

When Decheng was still small, Kong Yinqiu often invited him to sit in on meetings with the accountants or servants. After Decheng married at the age of seventeen, he formally took over the management of Mansion affairs, although he had actually been in charge before his marriage. At the time, Mansion affairs were in great disorder: there were many problems with the Mansion's five or six hundred servants and the records of rent payments by the Mansion's tenants were a hopeless mess. Decheng put much effort into reorganisation and instituted many reforms, of which a few are mentioned here:

1. He fixed regulations for attendance at work. In the past, Mansion servants came and went as they pleased in a highly informal manner. Decheng fixed working hours from seven to twelve in the morning and from two to five in the afternoon, and placed attendance registers at every workplace. Those with personal affairs to attend to had to apply for a day off and anyone who skipped work three times was fired. Those who punctually came to work each day for a fixed period were rewarded with a small quantity of dry grain.

2. Kong Mansion servants wore a rectangular cloth insignia with black characters on a white background, and each servant wore a number on his chest. After a fixed period, insignias were changed to prevent lost ones from being used by outsiders. This reduced the incidence of people masquerading as Kong Mansion staff in order to swindle and cheat unsuspecting victims.

3. Discipline was imposed on the servants, and responsibilities were fixed for each section of the Mansion. For example, the vat of water for dousing fires had to be kept full at all times; the courtyards had to be kept free of weeds; articles borrowed by guests had to be registered and returned after use; and antiques, paintings and calligraphy had to be protected. Servants had to walk in a sedate manner, and without special permission were not allowed to move freely around the Mansion.

4. The system of bonuses paid in grain was replaced by cash bonuses.

5. Decheng found that a dozen or so villages had not handed in their rent collection accounts. He stipulated that if they were not

submitted by a given date, those responsible would forfeit their positions.

6. He publicly announced that any labourer who broke the law would be fired and thus give up his exemption from government corvée labour.

7. An inventory of all objects in the Mansion was drawn up. Increases or decreases in staff members and the circulation of funds required Decheng's personal permission.

Decheng also made changes in his staff. There was a land manager named Chen Jingtang who my brother discovered was surreptitiously selling sacrificial fields. Decheng was furious and fired him immediately, but retained his brother Chen Jingrong as a personal attendant, not implicating him because of his brother's misdoings, as had been common in old China. There was also a servant named Ma Hai who frequently skipped work. As a punishment his grain ration was cut and he was temporarily removed from office. Conscientious workers received rewards and family members in financial difficulty were given financial aid. For such a young man to run the affairs of so large a family was certainly no easy task.

At that time many foreign guests came to the Mansion, the largest number of them from Japan. Before the Lugouqiao (Marco-Polo Bridge) Incident on July 7th, 1937,[1] the Japanese government sent men to Qufu to try to win Decheng over to their side to facilitate their invasion of China. The Japanese came to the Kong Mansion in a private capacity or for scholarly research and always in plain clothes. Sometimes they came singly and sometimes in large groups. The head of the Shanghai Natural Science Research Institute, Aranari Shinzo, came alone, while a party of fifty from the Qingdao Sports Association came all the way to Qufu expressly to pay their respects to Decheng. They were put up in the Hall of Loyalty and Forbearance. Japanese who had never met Decheng sent him gifts direct from Japan.

Baba Shunkichi was a Japanese who on his occasional visits to

---

[1] The incident was the prelude to the full-scale invasion of North China by the Japanese. Claiming that a soldier was missing, the local Japanese garrison demanded to search a town beside the famous bridge (built in 1192 with little carved lions on all the pillars, supposedly seen by Marco Polo in 1276) and took local resistance as a pretext for a blitzkrieg.

Qufu completed a 'Guide Map of the Sacred Relics' and a detailed survey of the Kong Mansion and Temple of Confucius – even recording the exact measurements of each gate. Afterwards he built a replica of the Temple of Confucius in Tokyo which he named the Hall of Cultural Refinement, after an inscription on a horizontal tablet in the Hall of Great Achievements in Qufu which read: 'Cultural Refinement May Be Found Here.' Many people came to Qufu for the express purpose of doing research on the architectural structure of the Mansion and Temple. The two who stayed longest and did the best work were the well known architect Liang Sicheng and the above-mentioned Baba Shunkichi.

In 1935, the Japanese government sent Kong Decheng, Meng Qingtang and the direct descendants of the other great Confucians, invitations to attend the opening ceremony for the Temple to Confucius in Japan. Analysing the situation at the time, it seemed likely that the Japanese would detain Decheng in custody, so he sent a member of the family named Kong Zhaorun to represent him. On his return, Zhaorun brought Decheng books and other gifts from the Japanese. Later, the Japanese sent a representative to Qufu to hold a banquet in Decheng's honour, but Decheng declined due to illness, and wrote a poem to express his thanks.

One evening in July 1937, Sun Tongxuan, the Commander of the Kuomintang 72nd Division stationed at Yanzhou, came to the Kong Mansion with an urgent telegram from Chiang Kai-shek advising Decheng to leave Qufu for Chongqing[1] immediately – if possible that very night. At this time, the Shandong Provincial Government was planning to move its offices to Qufu and several buildings in the Western College were prepared for their arrival and an air-raid shelter had been dug. But as Sun Tongxuan explained, the situation had changed. Once the main bridge over the Yellow River was destroyed, the Provincial Government planned to withdraw from Shandong immediately. Decheng was not willing to live under Japanese rule, but he was also reluctant to leave the Ancestral Temple without anyone to offer the sacrifices that had been maintained continuously for over 2,000 years. A sudden departure was

---

[1] Chongqing in remote western China was the seat of Chiang Kai-shek's government after the Japanese invasion. In 1945 his government moved back to its capital, Nanking, not far south of Qufu.

fraught with difficulties, but under the circumstances there was no choice.

An uncle of ours named Kong Shaguang, who had been Head of the Department of Finance in the Shandong Provincial Government, had moved to the Kong Mansion from Jinan just a month before. Decheng sent for him and asked him to act as State Master of Sacrifices on his behalf. One of my aunts, Madame Yuan, agreed to take responsibility for running the Inner Apartments, and other matters were entrusted to the clan head, the Council of the Clan members, and two of the schoolmasters, Wang Yuhua and Zhuang Gailan. Decheng's party had hoped to leave at 2 a.m., but it was four in the morning before they finally set off. They were accompanied by Sun Qifang's wet nurse, Decheng's teacher, Lü, Mother Zhang, and two personal attendants. They say that Sun Qifang was still having her hair done when they were about to leave, and she was hurried into the car with it only half done.

It wasn't until the next day that the staff and servants of the Kong Mansion learned that Decheng had left. The news reduced many of the old servants to sorrowful tears. At the time Sun Qifang was just about to give birth to a child.

When Decheng arrived at Wuhan, he issued an anti-Japanese statement, and when they were passing through Hubei Province, Sun Qifang gave birth to a daughter whom she named Kong Wei'e ('e' means Hubei Province). Upon their arrival in Chongqing, they stayed at Gele Mountain in a residence specially constructed for them by Chiang Kai-shek.

From Confucius to my brother Kong Decheng there stretched a direct line of seventy-seven generations, and throughout the centuries, only the forty-eighth generation descendant, Kong Ruiyou of the Southern Song dynasty, left Qufu to accompany the Song emperor to the south. But even then Kong Ruiyou's younger brother remained at Qufu to watch over the Ancestral Temple.

In August 1945, following the victory of the Anti-Japanese War, I received a letter from Decheng in Chongqing as well as a family portrait and letters from his daughter Wei'e and son Weiyi, both of them primary school students. That winter, my children and I vacationed in the south. We flew to Shanghai where Decheng and his secretary met us at the airport. He had made a special trip from Nanjing, which was again made the capital of China. The two of us had been separated for years and it was a moving reunion. Decheng embraced me and for a long time was unable to speak. I couldn't hold back my tears.

After staying in Shanghai for several days, we took a train to Nanjing together. Decheng lived in a little grey house in Langya Road, across the street from Shao Lizi, who was then the Kuomintang Minister for Propaganda, and Chen Cheng, a Kuomintang top general. Behind the residence was the Canadian Embassy. The environment was quiet and peaceful, but the atmosphere rather foreign. Nonetheless, Decheng's lifestyle still bore the imprint of the Kong Mansion. Despite the fact that American goods flooded the markets and most officials' wives dressed in modern clothing, my brother's wife still styled her hair in an old-fashioned bun and wore a traditional *cheongsam*. Decheng still wore a long scholar's gown. Their servants were the same people who had accompanied them from Qufu eight years before.

Besides the residence on Langya Road, Decheng rented one floor of a building in Sihaili near the Confucian Temple. Here he set up a Kong Decheng Affairs Agency where teachers Wang and Lü and several other office workers lived. Decheng received a monthly salary of 800 dollars which he had to use to cover daily living expenses, the cost of running the agency, as well as banquet and entertainment fees, so his financial situation was very tight. He didn't own a car and when we went out together had to borrow one from a friend. We arrived in Nanjing just as the Kuomintang government was holding important daily meetings, but he still found time to accompany me to Nanjing's major tourist spots and tried to be at home as often as possible to share meals with us.

Teacher Wang Yuhua had left Qufu to join Decheng in Nanjing, but Decheng sent him and Kong Lingshu back to the Mansion to take over from Kong Shaguang and organise a committee to administer the Kong Mansion. The secretary was Li Bingnan, and the committee members were Kong Luquan, Kong Lingshu, Kong Enting and Kong Chunjie. Decheng often held committee meetings at the Kong Decheng Affairs Agency to examine such problems as imposing levies on sacrificial fields and dealing out rewards and punishments to the Kong Mansion staff. They also discussed plans for raising money and allocated aid to clan members in need.

In 1948, Decheng decided to go to the United States to study and learn about American culture, and came to visit me in Suzhou, where I was living with my family, before he left. By the end of 1948, the political situation had become very tense. Decheng hastily returned home and made preparations to leave for Taiwan while I moved back to Nanjing.

It has now been thirty-two years since our separation, but recalling the early days I am still filled with unbounded affection for my brother. When will we meet again? If Taiwan could return to the motherland, that would bring about the earliest possible reunion.

7

My Hometown Revisited

It was forty years since I left home and not a single relative remained there, but memories of my childhood and a deep attachment to my native soil still tugged at my heartstrings. After the 'cultural revolution' I learned from the newspapers that the ancient relics damaged during those ten years of turbulence had been restored, and determined to go back and see it all with my own eyes. Although the thought that everyone in the Mansion would be strange to me made me somewhat hesitant, I nevertheless took my daughter Ke Lan, my son Ke Da, and my grandson Liu Yong and made the trip back home.

We were given a lavish welcome at Yanzhou where we disembarked and were taken to stay at the Kong Mansion. I woke early the next morning to the sound of birds calling outside the window. I listened carefully and told the children: 'There are still *wazi* in the trees!' *Wazi* was the local name for the small egrets which nested only in the tall trees inside the Kong Mansion. In my childhood I had loved them and after leaving home I dreamed about them.

I found the courtyards elegant and tranquil. They were now laid out attractively with flowers and trees, the green-glazed tiles on the curving eaves of the buildings and the carved and painted rafters and beams more eye-catching than ever in the bright morning sunshine. Strolling through the newly painted long corridor, I recalled the old days and described to the children each of the rooms and halls we passed.

In the Qianshang Building Courtyard, an old tree spread its branches like a great canopy, its masses of tiny white flowers assailing the nose with their fragrance. Years ago when we three children attended lessons in the Qianshang Building, the fragrance of these flowers wafting through the window in summer would make us lay down our brushes and run outside to play underneath its branches. The inkslabs we used in those days are still there on the table in the Qianshang Building. My hosts asked me to write something to commemorate my return visit. Unable to refuse, I picked up a writing brush and thought for a while. I hadn't written with a writing brush for a long time, and it felt like an iron pestle in my hand. The occasion inspired me to write down a famous poem by He Zhizhang of the Tang dynasty:

> Youthful I left my home and aged I return;
> The local accent remains unchanged but my hair is grey.
> Children I meet don't recognise my face;
> They smile and ask, 'Where has this guest come from?'

Everything inside the Kong Mansion was laid out very much as it had been in the old days. Calligraphy by my father Kong Lingyi and by Decheng decorated the walls of many rooms. Vertical scrolls and paired couplets have been reproduced and are now on sale in the local antique shop.

In the western room of the Qiantang Building hangs a portrait of my mother, Madame Wang. This was mother's bedroom, the room where we three children were born. A pair of desk clocks that stood on the table when we were born are still in perfect working order.

The east room of the Houtang Building remains unchanged from when Decheng lived there after his marriage. Sofas and desks still stand in their original places; the vases and the dressing table that were once part of Sun Qifang's dowry are still there. A photograph of Decheng and Sun Qifang with their children hangs on the wall in the inner bedroom. The photograph made me recall meeting Decheng at the Shanghai Airport after eight years of separation, for he looked then just as he did in this photograph.

In the courtyard of the Qiantang Building, where Decheng and I had lived together as children, the two pomegranate trees had grown tall and broad. They were heavy with fruit and the foliage was even more luxuriant than before. As children we had often gathered under these trees at the Mid-Autumn Festival to admire the moon and pick pomegranates. Now it was autumn again, and I was over sixty years old. I stood there alone, leaning on the tree trunk, gazing southwards and thinking of my relatives far away. Perhaps they were thinking the same thoughts – in the words of an ancient poet:

I raise my head to gaze at the bright moon,
Then lower my eyes and think of home.

Renovation of the Temple of Confucius had begun and work on the
Thirteen Tablet Pavilions, Hall of Poetry and Rites and many of the
halls and side rooms had already been completed. I stood before the
Apricot Altar gazing at the majestic Hall of Great Achievements
standing on its two-level terrace surrounded by a low marble
balustrade. I walked over to one of the balusters to the left of the
Hall and pointing to its carved top, said to the children: 'This pillar
looks like all the rest, but if you knock on it with your fist, it makes a
special sound. We call this the "sounding stone".' My grandson
knocked on it and went up close to listen. Sure enough, it emitted a
pleasant sound like that of a zither.

On another morning, we visited the Forest of Confucius. Our car
drove slowly along the newly laid road that circles the Forest and
came to a halt before my parents' grave. The grave is next to the
road, with ancient trees on three sides and an old stone altar
standing before it. The grave stone was smashed during the 'cultural
revolution', but has since been repaired with only a scar remaining
across its central section. In the morning mist, the gravestone was
covered with crystal drops of dew. I fell silent before the grave, my
heart surging with emotion, memories crowding into my mind . . .

After this we went to pay our respects at the grave of the founder
of the clan – Confucius. The Mount Tai commemorative tablet,
stone incense burners and stele inscribed by Huang Yangzheng were
all there undisturbed. Our guides told us that during the 'cultural
revolution', the local people were greatly distressed to see the tomb
and tablets smashed. The day the tomb was desecrated, some of
them came secretly in the night to collect the broken fragments and
hide them away. When Confucius' tomb was restored after the
destruction of the 'Gang of Four',[1] these people brought out the

[1] Name applied after their arrest in 1976 to Mao's wife, Jiang Qing, and her
associates Yao Wenyuan, Wang Hongwen and Zhang Chunqiao. Yao and
Zhang were political writers, Wang an ex-worker and leader of the rebels in
Shanghai during the Cultural Revolution and Jiang Qing an ex-actress. All were
associated with the extremist policies of the Cultural Revolution, arrested after
Mao died and tried in 1980, charged with perverting the Party and persecuting
individuals. All are still in prison, Jiang Qing and Zhang Chunqiao sentenced to
death (commuted), Wang and Yao to long sentences in prison.

broken fragments and the smashed relics were completely restored. There are many stories of ordinary people protecting cultural relics in this way: a peasant who was ordered to burn the gold-lettered horizontal tablet hanging over the Main Gate of the Kong Mansion hid the tablet until the Mansion was being renovated, when he brought it out and rehung it in its old place. There is also the story of the pair of stone lions that stand sentinel outside the Mansion gates. An official of Qufu County learned that they were going to be destroyed, and had a wooden box built around them on which he pasted the popular slogans of the time, thus saving them from destruction. These moving stories made me ponder: the people respect history and can correctly evaluate the past; they won't tolerate the denial of the rightful place that Confucius holds in the development of China's ancient culture.

Fellow townspeople from Qufu heard I had returned and welcomed me with great warmth, some even taking me by the hand and calling me by my childhood name. I was deeply moved. The townspeople hadn't forgotten me after all.

I lived at the Kong Mansion for a total of nearly twenty years. In those days, the worlds within and without the Mansion were completely separated from one another, and I had very little knowledge of the life of the people who lived beyond the Mansion's high walls. Out of curiosity, I would stand on a pile of earth inside the grounds, clinging to the top of the wall and secretly watch what went on outside, but apart from this I had few chances to experience life beyond the Main Gates. But now, after a few short days at home, I felt a strong mutual affinity with these townspeople. For the first time since the 'cultural revolution', I felt spiritually replenished, cheerful and optimistic.

Index

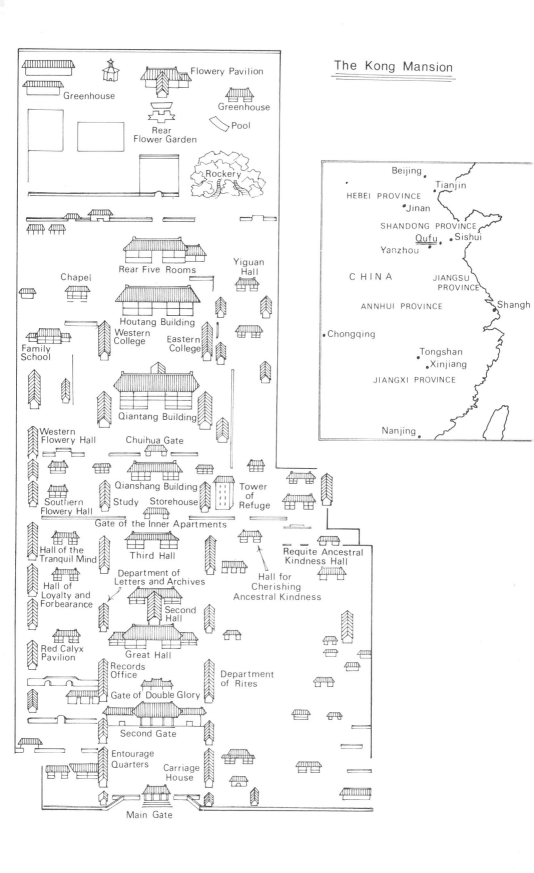

The Kong Mansion